Main Idea Activities
for English Language Learners and Special-Needs Students
with Answer Key

• •

THE **HOLT**
AMER
NATION
IN THE MODERN ERA

HOLT, RINEHART AND WINSTON
A Harcourt Education Company

Austin • New York • Orlando • Atlanta • San Francisco • Boston • Dallas • Toronto • London

Cover: National Air and Space Museum, Smithsonian Institution, Washington, DC.
Courtesy PRC.
Title Page: © CORBIS/Bill Ross

Printed in the United States of America

ISBN 0-03-065402-5

3 4 5 6 7 8 9   082   04 03 02

Main Idea Activities for Language Learners and Special-Needs Students

To the Teacher

Each section in the chapters of *The American Nation* has a corresponding set of main idea activities designed to meet the needs of students who are having difficulty understanding the section content or are continuing to acquire the English language. These activities use basic language and visuals to encourage mastery of specific objectives. Students can use completed main idea activities as study guides for future assessment.

CHAPTER 1

The New Nation

MAIN IDEA ACTIVITIES 1.1

■ VOCABULARY

Some terms to understand:

- **profound** (4): important; significant
- **edible** (4): suitable for eating
- **isolation** (5): separating oneself from other groups
- **merchants** (5): people who earn a living buying and selling goods
- **astrolabe** (6): tools used by navigators in the 1400s and 1500s to determine a ship's position by charting the position of the stars

■ ORGANIZING INFORMATION Complete the chart below about early Native American cultures using the following items.

- Aztec
- Inca
- Maya

- devised a number system and wrote with glyphs
- developed a canal system
- was the largest empire in the Americas

Group	Location	Achievements
•	Southern Mexico and Guatemala	•
•	Central Mexico	•
•	Andes of South America	•

■ EVALUATING INFORMATION Mark each statement *T* if it is true or *F* if it is false.

_____ **1.** The first people in the Americas crossed over a land bridge that at the time connected Asia and present-day Hawaii.

_____ **2.** Sometime between 10,000 and 5000 B.C., the climate in the Americas grew colder.

_____ **3.** The Agricultural Revolution increased the quantity and quality of food supplies.

_____ **4.** After the Mongols took over China, they made China the world's largest empire.

_____ **5.** Under feudalism, daily life centered around villages and the Roman Catholic Church.

_____ **6.** The Renaissance began in the 1900s in Italy and quickly spread to the rest of Europe.

_____ **7.** By the late 1500s the slave trade had become Portugal's major source of income.

_____ **8.** Vasco da Gama tried to reach Asia in 1492 by sailing west across the Atlantic Ocean.

_____ **9.** Queen Isabella protested the harsh treatment of Indians under the *encomienda* system.

_____ **10.** Spanish missionaries attempted to convert American Indians to Catholicism.

▓▓ REVIEWING FACTS Choose the correct item from the following list to complete the statements below.

Paleo-Indians	feudalism	*encomienda*
Agricultural Revolution	Crusades	Hernán Cortés
China	monarchies	Francisco Pizarro
Ghana		

1. The first Americans were called _____.

2. The _____ began when people started controlling plants and animals to meet human need.

3. The people of _____ invented paper and a system of printing.

4. In 772 an Arab geographer described _____ as "the land of gold."

5. Under _____, nobles pledged their loyalty and military assistance to more powerful leaders in return for land and protection.

6. The _____ were wars between Christians and Muslims for control of Jerusalem.

7. Near the end of the Middle Ages, national _____ replaced feudal kingdoms throughout most of western Europe.

8. Under the _____ system, American Indians suffered from over-work and malnutrition.

9. _____ conquered the Aztec and built Mexico City on the ruins of the Aztec capital.

10. The Inca resisted for several years before they finally fell to Spanish soldiers led by

_____.

The New Nation

MAIN IDEA ACTIVITIES 1.2

■ VOCABULARY

An expression to understand:

• **representative assembly (10):** small group of people chosen to represent the interests of a larger group in making rules or laws

Other terms:

• **cultivation (9):** the act of raising crops

• **seaboard (9):** land bordering a seacoast

• **refuge (12):** shelter; protection from danger or distress; a safe haven

• **pelts (14):** animal skins with the fur still attached

■ CLASSIFYING For each of the following, write the letter of the correct choice in the space provided.

_____ **1.** South Carolina   **a.** New England Colonies

_____ **2.** Georgia   **b.** Southern Colonies

_____ **3.** Connecticut   **c.** Middle Colonies

_____ **4.** Delaware

_____ **5.** North Carolina

_____ **6.** Maryland

_____ **7.** New York

_____ **8.** Providence, Rhode Island

_____ **9.** Plymouth Colony

_____ **10.** New Jersey

_____ **11.** Virginia

_____ **12.** Pennsylvania

_____ **13.** Massachusetts Bay Colony

■ EVALUATING INFORMATION Mark each statement *T* if it is true or *F* if it is false.

_____ **1.** Sir Walter Raleigh gave the name Carolina to the site on the Atlantic seaboard he chose to colonize.

_____ **2.** The Puritans wanted to purify the Church of England of all of its Catholic rituals and traditions.

_____ **3.** The New England Way involved a complete separation of church and state.

_____ **4.** Providence, Rhode Island, was founded by Anne Hutchinson.

_____ **5.** The Middle Passage was the voyage of enslaved Africans across the Atlantic Ocean to the Americas.

_____ **6.** In South Carolina, slaves made up nearly two thirds of the population.

_____ **7.** William Penn viewed his colony as a place where people of different nationalities and religious beliefs could live together peacefully.

_____ **8.** European settlers were very careful not to upset the American Indians' way of life.

■ UNDERSTANDING MAIN IDEAS For each of the following, write the letter of the *best* choice in the space provided.

_____ **1.** The Mayflower Compact created a
   a. new religion.
   b. self-governing colony.
   c. headright system.
   d. representative assembly.

_____ **2.** Which of the following was founded as a refuge for poor English settlers?
   a. Plymouth
   b. South Carolina
   c. New Jersey
   d. Georgia

_____ **3.** In 1675 Nathaniel Bacon led a group of rebels who burned
   a. Jamestown.
   b. Roanoke Island.
   c. Charles Town.
   d. New Netherland.

_____ **4.** What crop did Virginia and Maryland rely on heavily?
   a. cotton
   b. tobacco
   c. corn
   d. wheat

The New Nation

MAIN IDEA ACTIVITIES 1.3

■ VOCABULARY

Some terms to understand:

• **levied (15):** required by authority

• **abroad (20):** overseas

• **neutralize (22):** make powerless

■ CLASSIFYING INFORMATION Read the terms and the explanations below.
Match each statement with the document it represents.

Declaration of Independence	Treaty of Paris of 1763	Tea Act
Olive Branch Petition	Stamp Act	Coercive Acts
Declaratory Act	Treaty of Paris of 1783	Proclamation of 1763

1. It gave Canada, Spanish Florida, and most French land east of the Mississippi River to

   Britain. _____

2. It banned the settlement of lands west of the Appalachian Mountains.

   _____

3. It levied a tax on printed matter of all kinds. _____

4. It was passed by the British Parliament to assert full power and authority over the colonies.

   _____

5. It gave Britain a monopoly on the tea trade. _____

6. They were passed to punish colonists for the Boston Tea Party.

   _____

7. It stated the colonists' loyalty to the king and asked for his help in ending the conflict.

   _____

8. It was written to win support for independence, both at home and abroad.

   _____

9. It granted the United States the land from the Atlantic coast westward to the Mississippi

   River and from the Great Lakes south to Florida. _____

■ **EVALUATING INFORMATION** Mark each statement *T* if it is true or *F* if it is false.

_____ 1. Pontiac wanted Indian nations to unite and attack French forts on the frontier.

_____ 2. Colonists objected to what they called "taxation without representation."

_____ 3. The "shot heard round the world" was fired in Lexington, Massachusetts.

_____ 4. The delegates at the Second Continental Congress chose Thomas Paine to lead the Continental Army.

_____ 5. *Common Sense* stirred up public support for the Revolution and called for the end of British rule.

_____ 6. The lack of a strong central government made the Patriot war effort particularly difficult.

_____ 7. Forces led by George Rogers Clark captured Vincennes and secured Illinois country.

_____ 8. George Washington surrendered to General Cornwallis after the Battle of Yorktown.

■ **REVIEWING FACTS** Choose the correct item from the following list to complete the statements below.

Paul Revere	Paris	Boston Tea Party
Samuel Adams	Boston Massacre	Thomas Jefferson
Saratoga	Trenton	

1. _____ was a leader of the Boston Sons of Liberty.

2. In 1770 an argument between colonists and Redcoats led to the death of five people in what the colonists called the _____.

3. During the _____, colonists threw 342 chests of tea into Boston Harbor.

4. _____ and two other men sounded the alarm that the British were coming.

5. _____ did most of the actual writing of the Declaration of Independence.

6. The Patriots' victory at _____ was their first major offensive attack.

7. The victory at _____ persuaded Spain and France to ally with the Patriots.

8. The signing of the Treaty of _____ ended the Revolutionary War.

CHAPTER
1

The New Nation

MAIN IDEA ACTIVITIES 1.4

■ VOCABULARY

An expression to understand:

• **followed suit (29):** did the same thing

Other terms:

• **void (28):** emptiness
• **tracts (29):** defined areas of land
• **precedent (30):** something said or done that may serve as an example or rule at a later date
• **stability (32):** balance; steadiness, strength

■ ORGANIZING INFORMATION Complete the chart below about U.S. plans of government, using the following items.

• created a government based on federalism
• Shays's Rebellion revealed its weaknesses
• two-house legislature
• went into effect in 1788

• proposed changes required consent of 13 states
• created three branches of government
• went into effect in 1781
• one-house legislature

Articles of Confederation	U.S. Constitution
• _____ _____	• _____ _____
• _____ _____	• _____ _____
• _____ _____	• _____ _____
• _____ _____	• _____ _____

■ EVALUATING INFORMATION Mark each statement *T* if it is true or *F* if it is false.

_____ **1.** Under republicanism, leaders receive their authority from the citizens.

_____ **2.** Under the Articles, government could borrow and coin money, conduct foreign affairs, set policy toward American Indians, and settle disputes between states.

_____ **3.** One cause of the depression that occurred in 1784 was the loss of French markets.

_____ **4.** The Virginia Plan proposed a bicameral legislature.

_____ **5.** The Three-Fifths Compromise stated that only three fifths of the slave population would count in determining total state population.

_____ **6.** Federalists feared a strong national government.

_____ **7.** The U.S. Constitution has remained effective for more than 400 years.

_____ **8.** The elastic clause has increased the flexibility of the Constitution.

■ UNDERSTANDING MAIN IDEAS For each of the following, write the letter of the *best* choice in the space provided.

_____ **1.** Which of the following is a power of the state governments?
  a. coin money
  b. conduct elections
  c. raise armed forces
  d. establish foreign policy

_____ **2.** The legislative branch of government
  a. applies the laws.
  b. interprets the laws.
  c. carries out the laws.
  d. makes the laws.

_____ **3.** Who developed the theory of natural rights?
  a. John Locke
  b. Benjamin Franklin
  c. James Madison
  d. Roger Sherman

_____ **4.** The Great Compromise focused on the issue of
  a. what to name the new nation.
  b. commerce.
  c. slavery.
  d. representation in Congress.

_____ **5.** Federalists favored
  a. a weak national government.
  b. ratification of the Constitution.
  c. states' rights.
  d. monarchies.

_____ **6.** How many states had to ratify the Articles for it to take effect?
  a. 7
  b. 9
  c. 13
  d. 27

CHAPTER
2

The Expanding Nation

MAIN IDEA ACTIVITIES 2.1

■ VOCABULARY

Some expressions to understand:

• **opened the ballots (70):** took a look at how people voted

• **transition of power (75):** transfer of power from one person to another

Other terms:

• **prohibited (70):** forbidden; not allowed

• **advocated (70):** supported; promoted; argued for

• **uniform (72):** standardized; unchanging; constant

• **aristocratic (75):** refined; stately; well-bred

• **abandoned (75):** given up; let go; left behind

• **backfired (78):** had the opposite of the expected or planned outcome

• **key (78):** important; significant

■ ORGANIZING INFORMATION Complete the chart with information about the first political parties in the United States.

First Political Parties

Party	Federalists	
Leaders		Thomas Jefferson and James Madison
Beliefs	strong national government; favored commerce, particularly with Britain	

▪ EVALUATING INFORMATION Mark each statement *T* if it is true or *F* if it is false.

_____ **1.** George Washington was the first president of the United States.

_____ **2.** The Bill of Rights guarantees U.S. citizens specific rights.

_____ **3.** Alexander Hamilton advised Congress to strengthen the nation's credit by printing more money.

_____ **4.** France angered U.S. officials by kidnapping American sailors and forcing them to serve in the French navy.

_____ **5.** Congress passed the Alien and Sedition Acts to allow the president to imprison dangerous foreigners.

_____ **6.** Thomas Jefferson became the third president of the United States.

_____ **7.** John Marshall was selected as the Chief Justice of the United States.

_____ **8.** The power of the U.S. Congress to declare an act of the Supreme Court unconstitutional is known as judicial review.

_____ **9.** Thomas Jefferson and John Marshall both believed in the loose construction of the U.S. Constitution.

_____ **10.** To fulfill his promise of moderation, President Jefferson left some Federalist programs, such as the National Bank, untouched.

_____ **11.** The Louisiana Purchase was the smallest land deal in history.

_____ **12.** Meriwether Lewis and William Clark were hired to explore and map the Louisiana Territory.

_____ **13.** A Shoshone woman named Sacagawea provided invaluable help to the Lewis and Clark expedition.

_____ **14.** Congress passed the Embargo Act of 1807 to stop all shipments of American products to foreign ports.

_____ **15.** A Shawnee leader named Tecumseh tried to build a confederation of American Indian nations.

_____ **16.** In 1812 the United States declared war on Great Britain.

_____ **17.** British and U.S. relations worsened in the years following the war.

The Expanding Nation

MAIN IDEA ACTIVITIES 2.2

■ VOCABULARY

Some terms to understand:

- **canals (80):** waterways built for shipping or travel
- **locomotives (80):** trains
- **secede (81):** to withdraw from an organization
- **temperance (83):** avoiding any use of alcoholic beverages

■ EVALUATING INFORMATION Mark each statement *T* if it is true or *F* if it is false.

_____ **1.** After the War of 1812 Americans' nationalism declined.

_____ **2.** Transportation was a major problem in the early 1800s.

_____ **3.** New transportation systems developed under the American System made possible the creation of national markets.

_____ **4.** Few changes were made to the manufacturing industry during the 1800s.

_____ **5.** During the 1830s the largest group of immigrants came from Ireland.

_____ **6.** Irish immigrants were welcomed into the United States and lived prosperously.

_____ **7.** The cotton gin was a machine that made planting cotton easier.

_____ **8.** Most southern plantation owners owned 200 or more slaves.

■ REVIEWING FACTS Choose the correct items from the following list to complete the statements below.

American Anti-Slavery Society	Monroe Doctrine	Seneca Falls Convention
American System	nativism	strike
Indian Removal Act	Second Great Awakening	Underground Railroad
Missouri Compromise		

1. The _____ stated that the United States would oppose any European attempt to regain former Latin American colonies or to establish new ones in the Western Hemisphere.

2. Henry Clay proposed the _____ to establish stronger protective tariffs to encourage industrial development and fund a national transportation system.

3. The _____ admitted Missouri as a slave state and Maine as a free state.

4. The _____ required American Indians living in the East to relocate to Indian Territory in Oklahoma.

5. A(n) _____ is a refusal to work until employers meet union demands.

6. The favoring of native-born Americans over foreign-born residents is known as

   _____.

7. Many slaves escaped to freedom with help from a network of white and African American

   people called the _____.

8. During the 1790s there was a renewed and passionate interest in religion called the

   _____.

9. The _____ was dedicated to the end of slavery and fought for racial equality.

10. The _____ was held to discuss the rights of women.

■ UNDERSTANDING MAIN IDEAS For each of the following, write the letter of the *best* choice in the space provided.

_____ 1. Who was elected president as "a man of the people"?
   a. Henry Clay
   b. Andrew Jackson
   c. Frederick Douglass
   d. James Monroe

_____ 2. How many Cherokee people died on the march to Indian Territory known as the Trail of Tears?
   a. 40
   b. 400
   c. 4,000
   d. 40,000

_____ 3. In the early 1800s many young women held jobs in Lowell, Massachusetts, in
   a. hospitals.
   b. mills.
   c. steel factories.
   d. prisons.

_____ 4. Who led a slave revolt in 1831 that killed some 60 white people?
   a. Nat Turner
   b. Harriet Tubman
   c. Sojourner Truth
   d. Sarah Grimké

CHAPTER 2

The Expanding Nation

MAIN IDEA ACTIVITIES 2.3

■ VOCABULARY

An expression to understand:

• **coined the term (86):** made a phrase popular

Other terms:

• **fared (86):** turned out; did
• **descent (86):** background; ancestry; origin

■ ORGANIZING INFORMATION Complete the chart below about U.S.–Mexican relations in the 1800s, using the following items.

• Texas was granted independence in 1836.
• Mexico gave up all claims to Texas and surrendered the Mexican Cession.
• A conflict emerged regarding the border between Texas and Mexico.
• The Mexican government closed the Mexican border to Americans and President Santa Anna declared himself dictator.

U.S.–Mexican Border

War	Cause	Outcome
Texas Revolution	• _____ _____	• _____ _____
Mexican War	• _____ _____	• _____ _____

▨ EVALUATING INFORMATION Mark each statement *T* if it is true or *F* if it is false.

_____ 1. Thousands of families followed the Oregon Trail to the Pacific Northwest in the 1840s and 1850s.

_____ 2. Thousands of settlers traveled to California for its rich farming soil.

_____ 3. Texas was admitted to the Union as a slave state.

_____ 4. The Free-Soil Party wanted Congress to prohibit slavery in the new territories.

_____ 5. The Compromise of 1850 banned slavery in the District of Columbia.

_____ 6. The Kansas-Nebraska Act organized these new territories on the basis of popular sovereignty.

_____ 7. Stephen Douglas was elected president in the election of 1860.

_____ 8. South Carolina was the first state to secede from the Union.

▨ REVIEWING FACTS Choose the correct items from the following list to complete the statements below.

Dred Scott decision	Harriet Beecher Stowe	manifest destiny
Confederate States of America	John Brown	popular sovereignty

1. _____ was the belief that God intended the United States to expand westward to the Pacific Ocean.

2. _____ allowed the citizens of a new territory to vote whether to permit slavery.

3. _____ wrote *Uncle Tom's Cabin,* a book that convinced many Americans that slavery was morally wrong.

4. The Pottawatomie Massacre, in which five pro-slavery men were dragged from their beds and murdered, was led by _____.

5. The _____ declared that the federal government could not limit the spread of slavery.

6. The southern states that seceded from the Union formed the _____, with Jefferson Davis as provisional president.

Main Idea Activities

The Civil War

MAIN IDEA ACTIVITIES 3.1

■ VOCABULARY

Some expressions to understand:
- **torn apart (93):** separated; filled with tension
- **draw his sword (100):** fight in the war

Other terms:
- **inevitable (96):** unable to avoid; certain
- **preserve (96):** save

■ ORGANIZING INFORMATION Complete the chart by inserting these items next to the appropriate state or region.

- It was secured by federal troops in an effort to bar secession.
- It remained loyal to the Union.
- Because it had few slaves, its people sympathized with the North.
- Citizens were divided over the issue; the governor sympathized with the North so the state did not secede.
- Citizens were divided over the issue; the governor sympathized with the North so the state did not secede.
- Citizens fought on both sides of the war.

Positions of Border States and Regions on Secession

Delaware	
Kentucky	
Maryland	
Missouri	
Northwest Virginia	
Upper South	

■ CLASSIFYING INFORMATION Identify these items as northern advantages or southern advantages. Mark each blank with either *N* (northern) or *S* (southern).

_____ 1. had a larger population

_____ 2. only had to protect its property

_____ 3. had most of the nation's railroad lines

_____ 4. excellent military leadership

_____ 5. more resources

_____ 6. had a loyal Navy

■ EVALUATING INFORMATION Mark each statement *T* if it is true or *F* if it is false.

_____ 1. The Crittenden Compromise was proposed as an attempt to save the Union.

_____ 2. The Crittenden Compromise called for the old Missouri Compromise line to be drawn west through the remaining territories. North of the line slavery would be illegal; south of the line slavery could expand.

_____ 3. President Lincoln supported the Crittenden Compromise.

_____ 4. Lincoln supported protecting slavery where it already existed.

_____ 5. The Confederacy took over many federal arsenals, forts, and mints on Union lands.

_____ 6. Control of Fort Sumter was very important to the South, because it needed the fort to control access to a major port.

_____ 7. After 34 hours of fighting, Fort Sumter surrendered to the Confederate army.

_____ 8. Thirteen people were killed during the fighting at Fort Sumter.

_____ 9. President Lincoln called for 75,000 soldiers to put down the uprising in the South.

_____ 10. Some officials in France and Britain hoped the South would win, because they thought a divided United States would be less threatening to Europe.

_____ 11. Russia supported the South.

_____ 12. American Indians and African Americans fought in both armies.

_____ 13. The cotton plant was the symbol of the federal government.

_____ 14. The First Battle of Bull Run caused each side to seriously train its troops.

_____ 15. After the first Battle of Bull Run, the South felt secure and the North was more determined.

CHAPTER
3

The Civil War

MAIN IDEA ACTIVITIES 3.2

■ VOCABULARY

An expression to understand:
- **feeling like larks (103):** happy

Other terms:
- **strategy (103):** plan
- **penetrate (103):** move into

■ CLASSIFYING INFORMATION Identify these goals and strategies as that of the North or the South. Mark each blank with either *N* (North) or *S* (South).

_____ **1.** restore the Union

_____ **2.** capture Washington

_____ **3.** capture Richmond

_____ **4.** institute a naval blockade of the South

_____ **5.** gain control of the Mississippi River

_____ **6.** defend its home territory

■ ORGANIZING INFORMATION Fill in the Venn diagram by placing the items listed below in the correct parts of the diagram: North, South, and Both.

- Women worked as clerks in the Treasury Department.
- Women held patriotic events to urge young men to join the army.
- Female schoolteachers educated former slaves.
- Women held raffles to raise funds for the army.
- Women replaced male workers who were fighting in the war.

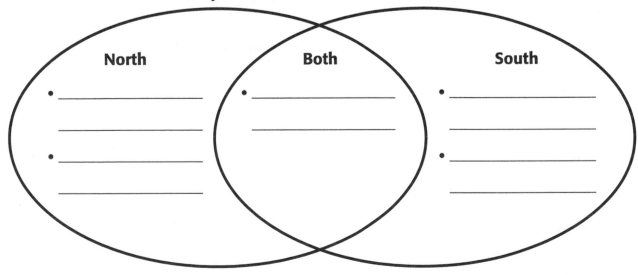

Responsibilities on the Home Front

North

Both

South

Main Idea Activities 3.2, Continued

◼ REVIEWING FACTS Choose the correct items from the following list to complete the statements below.

Anaconda Plan	Copperheads	shortages
Andersonville, Georgia	farmers	spies
Clara Barton	gray	Sally Louisa Tompkins
blue	illness	Union Draft Law
Catholic nuns	Mississippi River	Loreta Janeta Velázquez
Confederate		

1. The North's naval blockade of the South was called the _____ because it was meant to slowly squeeze the life out of the South.

2. Control of the _____ would enable the North to penetrate deep into the South and prevent the Confederacy from using the waterway to resupply its forces.

3. Both sides had _____ of clothing, food, and rifles.

4. The Union uniforms were _____.

5. The Confederate uniforms were _____.

6. The _____ army lacked good shoes and warm coats.

7. Thousands of soldiers died from _____.

8. The worst prisoner of war camp was in _____.

9. _____ disguised herself as a man and enlisted in the Confederate army.

10. Some women served as _____.

11. _____ were the only group allowed to move freely between Union and Confederate lines.

12. _____ was a nurse who founded the American Red Cross after the war.

13. _____ was the only recognized female officer in the Confederate forces.

14. The southern draft placed the major burden for fighting on poor

_____ and working people.

15. Many white working-class men opposed the _____.

16. Northern Democrats who sympathized with the South were called

_____.

18 Chapter 3

Main Idea Activities

Copyright © by Holt, Rinehart and Winston. All rights reserved.

CHAPTER 3

The Civil War

MAIN IDEA ACTIVITIES 3.3

■ VOCABULARY

Some expressions to understand:

• **finish off** (110): complete the battle

• **set ablaze** (111): set on fire

• **dragged on** (113): continued slowly

• **great slaughter pen** (117): a place where many people died

Other terms:

• **grasped** (110): understood

• **reinforcements** (110): more troops to help with the fighting

• **counterattack** (111): a return attack

• **pitch** (111): a dark, sticky tar

• **chronicle** (111): to record

• **outflank** (117): to go around and behind the side of the troops

■ EVALUATING INFORMATION Mark each statement *T* if it is true or *F* if it is false.

_____ **1.** During 1862 the Union won most of the major battles in the East.

_____ **2.** The Union's eastern forces had four different commanders in just one year.

_____ **3.** General Ulysses S. Grant was the leader of the Confederate forces in the West.

_____ **4.** The Union's victory at Shiloh gave the North a great advantage in the fight to control the Mississippi River valley.

_____ **5.** General McClellan trained his men well but often hesitated to commit his men to battle.

_____ **6.** African Americans were never allowed to serve in the Union army.

_____ **7.** President Lincoln could legally abolish slavery.

_____ **8.** General Lee's defeat at the Battle of Antietam cost the South any hope of support from European countries.

▆ REVIEWING FACTS Choose the correct items from the following list to complete the statements below.

54th Massachusetts Infantry	Battle of Antietam	Emancipation Proclamation
African American	Battle of Shiloh	Seven Days' Battles

1. On April 6, 1862, thousands of Confederate troops surprised General Grant's soldiers,

   beginning the _____.

2. The _____ was considered a victory for the South because General McClellan retreated.

3. President Lincoln's _____ freed all slaves living in areas still rebelling against the United States.

4. The Union's victory at the _____ was the bloodiest single-day battle in all of U.S. military history.

5. Many African American Union soldiers served in the _____.

6. The attack on Fort Wagner represented the first time that _____ troops had been assigned a key role in a military campaign.

▆ UNDERSTANDING MAIN IDEAS For each of the following, write the letter of the best choice in the space provided.

_____ 1. Which of these was not a key factor in the Union's control of Kentucky and much of Tennessee?
   a. Fort Henry
   b. Fort Pierre
   c. Fort Donelson
   d. Nashville

_____ 2. Union control of the Mississippi depended on taking _____, the largest city in the South.
   a. Memphis
   b. Nashville
   c. Richmond
   d. New Orleans

_____ 3. President Lincoln fired
   a. McClellan.
   b. Lee.
   c. Grant.
   d. Delany.

_____ 4. In 1865 Martin Delany became the first African American promoted to the rank of
   a. general.
   b. sergeant.
   c. corporal.
   d. major.

_____ 5. More than 20 African American soldiers won the Congressional Medal of Honor. Which of the pictures shows that award?

a.

c.

b.

d.

★
★★
CHAPTER
3

The Civil War

MAIN IDEA ACTIVITIES 3.4

■ VOCABULARY

Some terms to understand:

• **ashen (118):** light gray; white

• **invincible (118):** unable to be beaten

■ ORGANIZING INFORMATION To complete the calendar below, insert these items under the correct day.

• General Lee ordered 15,000 men to rush the Union center on Cemetery Ridge.

• The Confederates pushed the Union line back to Cemetery Hill and Cemetery Ridge.

• General Lee charged the Union's left flank, but did not capture Little Round Top.

July 1863

1	2	3

■ REVIEWING FACTS Choose the correct items from the following list to complete the statements below.

Appalachian Mountains	William T. Sherman	total war
Chancellorsville	Siege of Vicksburg	war of attrition
Gettysburg Address		

1. Following the victory at _____, General Lee decided to invade the North again.

2. President Lincoln helped dedicate a cemetery at the Gettysburg battlefield. It was there that

he delivered his famous speech, the _____.

3. During the _____, the Confederate army had to eat mules and
rats to keep from starving.

4. A _____ is a plan to continue fighting until the enemy runs out
of men, supplies, and the will to go on.

5. General _____ undertook a campaign to destroy southern railroads and industries.

6. When Atlanta fell, the Confederates lost their last railroad link across the

_____.

7. Some believe that to win a war you must strike at the enemy's economic resources as well as

their troops. This is called fighting a _____.

▬ UNDERSTANDING MAIN IDEAS For each of the following, write the letter of the *best* choice in the space provided.

_____ **1.** General Grant knew that gaining
full control of the Mississippi
River required taking
   a. New Orleans.
   b. Richmond.
   c. Tallahassee.
   d. Vicksburg.

_____ **2.** Which of these was not a term of
Lee's surrender?
   a. Confederate officers could
keep their side arms.
   b. All soldiers would be fed and
allowed to keep their horses
and mules.
   c. All soldiers would become servants of the Union army.
   d. No one would be tried for
treason.

_____ **3.** Which of these proved to be
helpful to President Lincoln's
re-election campaign?
   a. the Mexican War
   b. the Emancipation
Proclamation
   c. the Gettysburg Address
   d. the fall of Atlanta

_____ **4.** Lincoln promoted _____ to
commander of all Union forces in
the spring of 1864.
   a. McClellan
   b. Grant
   c. Lee
   d. Pemberton

CHAPTER 4 Reconstruction and the New South

MAIN IDEA ACTIVITIES 4.1

◼ VOCABULARY

Some expressions to understand:

- **in ruins (130):** destroyed
- **droves of people (130):** large groups of people
- **frame of reference (132):** a way of looking at one thing based on knowledge or experience of something else
- **iron hand (132):** a heavy and inflexible control over something
- **laid down their arms (132):** stopped fighting

Other terms:

- **jubilee (130):** a celebration
- **proclamation (131):** an official public announcement
- **conspiracy (132):** a plan by a group of people to do something wrong or illegal
- **assumed (133):** took over
- **nullify (133):** to take away something's importance or value
- **adequate (134):** enough to meet a need
- **denounce (134):** to say openly that something is evil or shameful

◼ ORGANIZING INFORMATION Complete the chart by listing what President Johnson did in reaction to complaints of southerners during Reconstruction.

President Johnson's Reactions to Southern Complaints

- _____
  _____
- _____
  _____

◼ EVALUATING INFORMATION Mark each statement *T* if it is true or *F* if it is false.

_____ **1.** President Lincoln had taken the Union into war because he wanted to destroy the South.

_____ **2.** The Civil War improved the South's economy.

_____ **3.** With the end of the Civil War, freedpeople hoped to have the same rights as other citizens.

_____ **4.** President Lincoln, President Johnson, and Congress agreed on the same plan for Reconstruction.

_____ **5.** President Johnson believed that only white citizens should control the government.

_____ **6.** Many northerners believed President Lincoln's assassination was a conspiracy by Confederate leaders.

_____ **7.** The Black Codes were not very different than southern pre–Civil War slave codes.

■■ **REVIEWING FACTS** **Choose the correct items from the following list to complete the statements below.**

Black Codes	Proclamation of Amnesty	President Andrew Johnson
John Wilkes Booth	and Reconstruction	African Americans
Wade-Davis Bill	Sidney George Fisher	
Alexander H. Stevens	Thirteenth Amendment	

1. The _____ abolished slavery against the law.

2. President Lincoln hoped the _____ would persuade southerners to give up the Confederacy and rejoin the Union.

3. Congress presented the _____, which would not allow Reconstruction to begin until a majority of white males in the Confederate states made a formal promise that they would be loyal to the Union.

4. Southerners supported _____'s plan for Reconstruction because it would allow former Confederate lawmakers to control the types of laws that would be in the new state constitutions.

5. On April 14, 1865, _____ shot President Lincoln, making it easier for President Johnson to begin his own Reconstruction plan.

6. Like many other ordinary Americans, _____ believed Lincoln's death would allow certain northerners to take revenge on the South.

7. The southern states succeeded in greatly limiting the freedom of former slaves by creating

the _____.

8. President Johnson's policies allowed former Confederate vice president

_____ to take office as a representative.

9. The Black Codes allowed southern whites to control the labor of

_____ again.

Reconstruction and the New South

MAIN IDEA ACTIVITIES 4.2

■ VOCABULARY

Some expressions to understand:

- **unfavorable conditions (137):** a situation that is against someone's welfare
- **spree of violence (139):** wild and uncontrolled actions that are harmful to people and property

Other terms:

- **divisive (135):** causes a difference of opinion
- **bloated (136):** being bigger or more powerful than it should be
- **blueprint (136):** a plan of action
- **heed (138):** pay attention to
- **absurd (139):** silly and without good sense
- **alienated (142):** caused a person or group of people to turn against an idea or another person

■ ORGANIZING INFORMATION Complete the graphic organizer below by listing the following actions or events in the correct order.

- Congress passes Freedmen's Bureau Bill
- Congress passes Tenure of Office Act
- moderate and Radical Republicans join forces
- Congress passes Reconstruction Acts of 1867
- elections of 1866 give Republicans control of Congress
- Johnson removes Secretary of War Edwin Stanton
- Johnson vetoes Civil Rights Act of 1866
- Fourteenth Amendment passes
- Congress passes Civil Rights Act of 1866
- Johnson vetoes Freedmen's Bureau Bill

Moving Toward Impeachment

1. _____

2. _____

3. _____

4. _____

5. _____

6. _____

7. _____

8. _____

9. _____

10. _____

■ EVALUATING INFORMATION Mark each statement *T* if it is true or *F* if it is false.

_____ **1.** Frederick Douglass was a former slave who supported President Johnson's plans for Reconstruction.

_____ **2.** Pennsylvania representative Thaddeus Stevens wanted to use land reform to force changes in the structure of southern life.

_____ **3.** Moderate and Radical Republicans strongly disagreed on African American voting rights.

_____ **4.** One of the purposes of the Civil Rights Act of 1866 was to overturn the Supreme Court's decision in 1857 that African Americans were not citizens.

_____ **5.** The Fourteenth Amendment guaranteed African Americans the right to vote.

_____ **6.** The Reconstruction Acts of 1867 required the former Confederate states to ratify the Fourteenth Amendment before they could rejoin the Union.

_____ **7.** President Johnson escaped impeachment by a single vote.

_____ **8.** Republicans believed that the African American vote was the reason General Ulysses S. Grant won the presidential election of 1868.

_____ **9.** The Fifteenth Amendment extended to women the right to vote.

Reconstruction and the New South

MAIN IDEA ACTIVITIES 4.3

■ VOCABULARY

Some expressions to understand:

- **political leverage (144):** using political power to affect an action
- **white supremacy (146):** the belief that the white race is naturally of higher value than all other races and should be allowed to rule over all nonwhite races

Other terms:

- **lobbying (143):** trying to get a government or public official to act for or against a specific cause
- **renegades (144):** people who go against a group they used to belong to and then join another
- **corruption (145):** change that ends up destroying something
- **assertive (145):** bold; confident
- **reconvened (146):** came back together

■ ORGANIZING INFORMATION Complete the graphic organizer about what occurred as a result of the Panic of 1873, using the following items.

- Republicans agreed to withdraw remaining federal troops from the South.
- Republican Party's interest in universal voting rights faded.
- Democrats in some southern states used terrorism to prevent African Americans from voting for the Republican Party.
- Voters turned against the Republican-controlled Congress.
- Republicans abandoned universal voting rights.

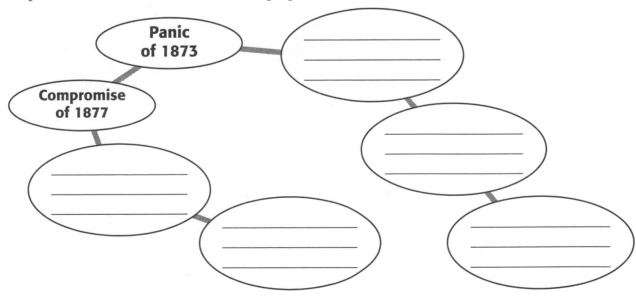

■ **REVIEWING FACTS** **Choose the correct items from the following list to complete the statements below.**

Union	Nathan Bedford Forrest	discriminating
vote	immigrants	Compromise of 1877
read	military	Panic of 1873
government		

1. The _____ League helped African Americans to become more active in politics so they could have greater control over their own futures.

2. During Reconstruction, many more African Americans learned to

   _____.

3. Republican state governments passed laws to make sure that white and African American

   men had the right to _____.

4. Former slave-trader and Confederate general _____ used his leadership of the Ku Klux Klan to frighten African Americans and to prevent them from supporting the Republicans.

5. The Enforcement Acts allowed the government to use the

   _____ to stop violence against African Americans.

6. When many _____ started to arrive in the United States, Republicans no longer supported the idea that all male citizens should vote.

7. The Democrats used the _____ to gain power in the House of Representatives.

8. The Redeemers acted to make sure that only whites controlled the

   _____.

9. The Civil Rights Act of 1875 was intended to prevent public businesses from

   _____ against African Americans.

10. The _____ between Democrats and Republicans took away federal support of the Reconstruction governments.

CHAPTER
4

Reconstruction and the New South

MAIN IDEA ACTIVITIES 4.4

■ VOCABULARY

An expression to understand:

• **color-blind (150):** not seeing differences in people based on race or class

Other terms:

• **disenfranchised (150):** took away their right to vote

• **cooperative (150):** groups of people who join together to buy something

• **ode (151):** a particular kind of poem

• **laurels (151):** a mark of honor

• **caulkers (152):** people who fill cracks in the side of a boat to prevent water from leaking in

■ ORGANIZING INFORMATION Complete the chart about the advantages and disadvantages of the sharecropping system, using the items below.

• farmers had a place to live

• led to the crop-lien system

• encouraged growing only one crop

• easy to build debt

• planters did not have to pay in cash

• workers got a portion of profit from crops

The Sharecropping System

Advantages	Disadvantages
• _____ _____	• _____ _____
• _____ _____	• _____ _____
• _____ _____	• _____ _____

◼ REVIEWING FACTS Choose the correct items from the following list to complete the statements below.

Ida B. Wells   Madame C. J. Walker   Homer Plessy
Jim Crow laws   Booker T. Washington   Henry W. Grady
cotton   cooperatives   Justice John Marshall Harlan

1. Sharecroppers suffered because their fortunes were tied to the

   _____ crop.

2. _____ believed that one-crop agriculture was the reason the
   South stayed economically poor and had to rely too much on the North for supplies.

3. The _____ were named after a minstrel song.

4. The Supreme Court ruled that the Fourteenth Amendment had not been violated when

   _____ was told he could not sit in the first-class railway car.

5. _____ believed that the Constitution did not allow citizens to
   be treated differently based on their race or what part of society they came from.

6. African Americans formed _____ to help themselves build
   schools, buy land, and provide for the aged.

7. Even though she worked in the cotton fields as a child, _____
   developed a successful business based on a special hair-conditioning treatment for African
   American women and became one of the first female millionaires in the United States.

8. As founder of the Tuskegee Institute in Alabama, _____
   believed that African Americans would achieve equality through economic independence.

9. _____ was a journalist and teacher who believed that African
   Americans should openly protest unfair treatment by southern whites.

CHAPTER
5

The Western Crossroads

MAIN IDEA ACTIVITIES 5.1

■ VOCABULARY

Some terms to understand:

• **mourned (162):** expressed sorrow about something

• **vision (165):** a mystical experience in which something is seen when it is not really there

• **battalion (165):** organized military troop

• **seizure (166):** the act of someone in authority taking something away from someone else

• **culmination (167):** an ending or completion

• **assimilation (168):** a process by which a minority group adopts the culture and ideas of a larger group and blends in with that group

• **silversmithing (169):** making or repairing objects made of silver

■ ORGANIZING INFORMATION Complete the graphic organizer that explains the United States's reservation system, using the items below.

• opened lands for settlement

• reduced size of reservations

• forced them to farm

• forced them to abandon their traditions

• Bureau of Indian Affairs

• forced them to move

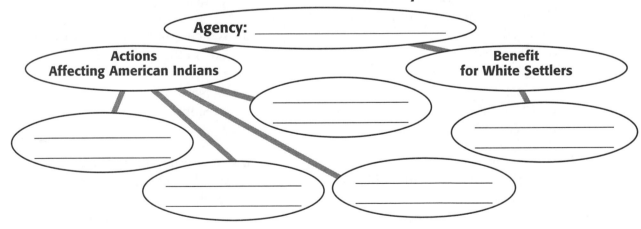

United States's Reservation System

Agency: _____

Actions Affecting American Indians

Benefit for White Settlers

■ EVALUATING INFORMATION Mark each statement *T* if it is true or *F* if it is false.

_____ 1. Bureau of Indian Affairs commissioner Luke Lea supported the reservation system.

_____ 2. Some treaties negotiated by the U.S. government promised American Indians yearly supplies for 30 years.

_____ **3.** The Cheyenne leader, Black Kettle, led his warriors against U.S. soldiers during the Battle of Sand Creek.

_____ **4.** U.S. Army colonel John M. Chivington was ashamed of his troops' actions at Sand Creek.

_____ **5.** The Treaty of Medicine Lodge promised the southern Plains Indians reservations in Indian Territory.

_____ **6.** Sitting Bull was a Sioux leader who was in favor of American Indians adopting the ways of the white man.

_____ **7.** In the Battle of the Little Bighorn, General George Armstrong Custer led 200 soldiers against about 2,500 American Indian warriors.

_____ **8.** The Nez Percé were less than 40 miles away from the Canadian border and freedom when Chief Joseph was forced to surrender.

▨ UNDERSTANDING MAIN IDEAS For each of the following, write the letter of the *best* choice in the space provided.

_____ **1.** Who was the Paiute Indian who first introduced the Ghost Dance religious movement?
- **a.** Cochise
- **b.** Geronimo
- **c.** Wovoka
- **d.** Sitting Bull

_____ **2.** Whose name was removed from the national monument at Little Bighorn?
- **a.** Crazy Horse
- **b.** General George Armstrong Custer
- **c.** Black Elk
- **d.** Colonel James Forsyth

_____ **3.** The last major incident between soldiers and Great Plains Indians was the
- **a.** Battle of the Rosebud.
- **b.** Battle of the Little Bighorn.
- **c.** Massacre at Wounded Knee.
- **d.** Battle of San Carlos.

_____ **4.** Who was the American Indian activist who persuaded President Rutherford B. Hayes to permit the Paiute to return to their homelands?
- **a.** Sarah Winnemucca
- **b.** Black Kettle
- **c.** Big Foot
- **d.** Black Coyote

_____ **5.** Which group was forced to take part in the Long Walk?
- **a.** Cheyenne
- **b.** Navajo
- **c.** Sioux
- **d.** Paiute

_____ **6.** The breaking up of reservation land by private ownership was the result of the
- **a.** Treaty of Fort Laramie.
- **b.** Treaty of Medicine Lodge.
- **c.** Long Walk.
- **d.** Dawes General Allotment Act.

The Western Crossroads

CHAPTER 5

MAIN IDEA ACTIVITIES 5.2

■ VOCABULARY

Some expressions to understand:

- **gain title to (170):** become the owner of
- **on credit (171):** buying something without paying for it right away
- **plough team (174):** two or more horses, mules, or oxen used to pull a plough

Other terms:

- **lured (171):** persuaded by promising a gift or reward
- **offset (171):** compensate for; provide a balance for
- **swales (174):** moist land that is lower than surrounding land
- **misgivings (174):** not being entirely sure about something
- **dreaded (175):** faced with horror

■ ORGANIZING INFORMATION Complete the chart below that explains the movement of people into the West after the Civil War.

Westward Movement After the Civil War

Group	Moved from	Reasons for Move
1. White Americans	_____	_____ _____ _____
2. _____	The South	_____
3. European Immigrants	_____ _____ _____ _____ _____	

■ UNDERSTANDING MAIN IDEAS For each of the following, write the letter of the *best* choice in the space provided.

_____ **1.** Which settlement act allowed settlers to own their land after living on it for five years?
  a. Homestead Act
  b. Morrill Act
  c. Pacific Railway Act
  d. Stamp Act

_____ **2.** Because of the cost of moving west from the eastern part of the United States, most white settlers from the East were
  a. very poor.
  b. middle class.
  c. wealthy.
  d. former slaveholders.

_____ **3.** The Kansas Fever Exodus of 1879 was
  a. an outbreak of yellow fever in Kansas.
  b. one of the biggest western settlement moves by African Americans.
  c. an incident during which Kansas lost half of its population.
  d. a settlers' song popular during the 1800s.

_____ **4.** Which government agency taught dry farming methods to help new farmers who were settling the Plains areas?
  a. U.S. Army
  b. Bureau of Indian Affairs
  c. U.S. Department of Agriculture
  d. House of Representatives

_____ **5.** Farming on the Great Plains was made very difficult by its harsh climate and plant-eating
  a. buffalo.
  b. birds.
  c. deer.
  d. insects.

_____ **6.** Special windmills that could stand up in the strong Plains winds were used to
  a. find oil.
  b. generate electricity.
  c. forecast weather.
  d. draw water from wells.

The Western Crossroads

MAIN IDEA ACTIVITIES 5.3

◼ VOCABULARY

Some expressions to understand:

- **chuck wagon (178):** a wagon pulled by horses or mules that contained equipment needed for making food
- **branding cattle (180):** using a red-hot iron tool to burn a special mark on the hide of a cow
- **supply far exceeded demand (181):** had more of something than was wanted or could be sold

Other terms:

- **depot (177):** a place where things could be brought together and then sent out again in many different directions
- **immune (177):** had a natural resistance
- **romanticized (178):** based on imagination rather than on fact
- **stampcdc (178):** a group of frightened animals running quickly in one direction
- **temperance (179):** very little or no use of alcohol
- **hammered (182):** hit over and over again

◼ EVALUATING INFORMATION Mark each statement *T* if it is true or *F* if it is false.

_____ 1. John Muir called sheep hoofed locusts because he believed that they destroyed grazing areas that cattle could use.

_____ 2. African American cowboys suffered less discrimination than other African Americans in the years after the Civil War.

_____ 3. Mexican cowboys were respected by the white cowboys and were often asked to be herd bosses.

_____ 4. Towns grew around the cities where railway lines were used to ship cattle to the East and further west.

_____ 5. The open-range system encouraged investors to create huge ranches.

_____ 6. On cattle and sheep ranches, women helped mend fences, cooked for all the cowboys, and did housework.

■ UNDERSTANDING MAIN IDEAS For each of the following, write the letter of the *best* choice in the space provided.

_____ 1. Sheep ranchers and cattle ranchers
   a. helped each other prosper.
   b. fought each other.
   c. worked on the same ranch.
   d. immigrated from Canada.

_____ 2. Cattle were most often driven to the railway lines in which state?
   a. Louisiana
   b. Wisconsin
   c. Kansas
   d. Texas

_____ 3. Who was the western artist who had a more realistic view of what happened to American Indians upon the arrival of settlers?
   a. Charles Russell
   b. Frederic Remington
   c. Eliza Barchus
   d. James Whistler

_____ 4. As more and more families arrived, cattle towns began to build
   a. saloons.
   b. bathhouses.
   c. schools.
   d. hitching posts.

_____ 5. A ranch could not survive unless the cattle or sheep could easily get to
   a. a veterinarian.
   b. fenced corrals.
   c. special food.
   d. water.

_____ 6. What was often used by farmers and ranchers to control the use of their land and water?

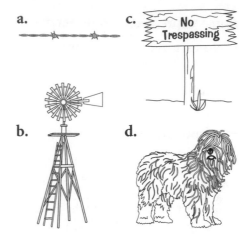

_____ 7. As the cattle boom ended, some ranchers learned that it was important to
   a. file land deeds with the government.
   b. raise sheep and cattle together.
   c. grow their own hay to feed cattle.
   d. use more cowboys on cattle drives.

_____ 8. One of the reasons sheep ranching was still profitable even after the cattle boom was because sheep
   a. were smaller.
   b. could eat weeds as well as grass.
   c. did not stampede.
   d. were easier to transport.

CHAPTER
5

The Western Crossroads

MAIN IDEA ACTIVITIES 5.4

◼ VOCABULARY

Some expressions to understand:

- **happy-go-easy (183):** a kind of person who is in a happy mood most of the time and does not have a serious attitude toward life

- **economic boom (183):** a period of time when the economy becomes very prosperous very quickly

- **strike it rich (183):** to suddenly become very wealthy

- **vigilante committees (185):** volunteer groups of citizens who give themselves the authority to punish those they consider guilty of doing something wrong

Other terms:

- **exaggerated (183):** described something as bigger, better, or more important than it really is

- **brawls (185):** noisy fights involving several people at once

- **scavenged (186):** searched through something after it has already been looked at or worked with

- **corps (187):** a special group of people acting together to achieve a particular goal

- **respiratory (187):** systems and organs that affect breathing

◼ CLASSIFYING INFORMATION Mark each of the following terms with *B* (Before) if it was part of a mining camp before the arrival of families or *A* (After) if it was a part of a mining camp after the arrival of families.

_____ **1.** theaters

_____ **2.** mainly tents to live in

_____ **3.** almost all of the people living in the town were men

_____ **4.** churches

_____ **5.** newspapers

_____ **6.** a greater variety of food to eat

■ REVIEWING FACTS Choose the correct items from the following list to complete the statements below.

arguments over claims	Klondike Gold Rush	breathe
union	mining camps	Cripple Creek
William Kelley	Hispanic	hydraulic mining

1. The patio mining process was a method introduced by _____ miners in Arizona.

2. Almost 100,000 people passed through the state of Alaska during the

   _____ .

3. In Colorado, eastern and southern Europeans and Hispanics were forced out of the

   _____ camp.

4. In the early mining camps, _____ caused many violent fights among miners.

5. Denver, Colorado, and Carson City, Nevada, were _____ before they became large towns.

6. _____ methods caused particularly bad damage to the environment.

7. Because there was very little fresh air deep in mine tunnels, miners developed many illnesses

   that affected their ability to _____ .

8. The Supreme Court decided that even though _____ was blinded in a mining accident, the mining company did not have to pay him any money.

9. Better wages for miners and help for miners' families were two achievements of the

   _____ that miners formed to help themselves.

■ INTERPRETING VISUAL IMAGES
Examine the drawing and answer the questions below.

1. What is the device the men are using?

   _____

2. Why are they using this device?

   _____

3. Where did this activity take place?

   _____

CHAPTER 6 The Second Industrial Revolution

MAIN IDEA ACTIVITIES 6.1

■ VOCABULARY

Some terms to understand:

- **exposition (192):** a public show that features new ideas in art or technology
- **spur (192):** to encourage action
- **skeletal frame (193):** the interior structure that supports a building
- **groundwork (194):** basic idea or object upon which other things are built
- **innovations (195):** new ideas
- **piloted (196):** controlled or led
- **marvel (197):** something that is wonderful and amazing

■ ORGANIZING INFORMATION Complete the graphic organizer about innovations during the Second Industrial Revolution, using the following items.

- Drake's Folly
- American steel production increased dramatically
- could be turned into kerosene
- process to refine oil
- Bessemer process
- Holley's adaptation
- produced more steel in a day than previously produced in a week
- flow of oil from well at vastly increased rate

Innovations of the Second Industrial Revolution

Innovation	Result
Steel	
1. _____ →	_____
2. _____ →	_____
Oil	
3. _____ →	_____
4. _____ →	_____

■ **UNDERSTANDING MAIN IDEAS** For each of the following, write the letter of
the *best* choice in the space provided.

_____ 1. Because of its value, oil was often
called
   a. black diamonds.
   b. liquid money.
   c. black gold.
   d. slick cash.

_____ 2. What was one of the important
developments in railroad track
design that made transporting
people and freight easier?
   a. standard rail gauge
   b. steam engine
   c. air brakes
   d. electrical wiring

_____ 3. Who was the French artillery officer who used a steam engine to
create the first horseless carriage?
   a. Thomas Alva Edison
   b. Nikolas Tesla
   c. Samuel F. B. Morse
   d. Nicolas-Joseph Cugnot

_____ 4. What new invention did the
Wright brothers use for the first
working airplane?
   a. fiberglass
   b. gasoline engine
   c. telegraph
   d. electric light bulb

_____ 5. People began to see what an
important invention the telegraph
was when they thought about
how to use it in
   a. education.
   b. entertainment.
   c. business.
   d. church.

_____ 6. The talking telegraph was another
name for the
   a. gasoline-powered engine.
   b. kerosene lamp.
   c. telegram.
   d. telephone.

_____ 7. The invention of the typewriter
led to many occupations for
   a. women.
   b. doctors.
   c. Civil War veterans.
   d. politicians.

_____ 8. Who was the inventor who
promised to deliver "a minor
invention every ten days or so
and a big thing every six months
or so"?
   a. Elijah McCoy
   b. Alexander Graham Bell
   c. Thomas Alva Edison
   d. George Westinghouse

_____ 9. Where was one of the first electric
power plants in the United States
located?
   a. Detroit, Michigan
   b. San Francisco, California
   c. New York City, New York
   d. Chicago, Illinois

_____ 10. Because of all the twinkling lights
on the buildings, the 1893
World's Columbian Exposition
was called the
   a. Star Palace.
   b. Wonder World.
   c. Dreamland.
   d. White City.

The Second Industrial Revolution

MAIN IDEA ACTIVITIES 6.2

■ VOCABULARY

Some expressions to understand:

- **self-reliant individualism (201):** depending only on yourself to achieve your own goals

- **rags-to-riches (201):** going from great poverty to great wealth

- **steel baron (202):** an important and rich person in the steel industry

- **board of trustees (203):** group of people who manage and control the direction of a business

- **pay a royalty (204):** pay the author or inventor a share of the profits from the sale of his or her work

Other terms:

- **capital (203):** money

- **ruthless (204):** having no mercy or pity

- **relentlessly (204):** without stopping to rest

- **tycoon (205):** a wealthy and powerful businessman

- **feudalism (207):** a medieval political and social system in which one person owns all the property and everyone who lives on the property must work for that person and live according to that person's rules

■ ORGANIZING INFORMATION List the leader of American industry associated with the product in each drawing.

American Industry Leaders

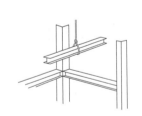  

1. _____   2. _____   3. _____

■ EVALUATING INFORMATION Mark each statement *T* if it is true or *F* if it is false.

_____ **1.** Many social Darwinists believed that giving direct help to the poor or less capable worker was required for social progress.

_____ **2.** Because a trust managed a number of corporations as one business, trusts enabled corporations to have almost total control over the price and quality of a product.

_____ **3.** Andrew Carnegie's real success in the steel industry was due to his ability to keep the costs of making goods as low as possible.

_____ **4.** Believers in the Gospel of Wealth felt that they had no responsibility to use their success to improve society.

_____ **5.** George Westinghouse made his fortune through the invention of the refrigerator.

_____ **6.** Brightly colored packages, distinctive names, and logos were marketing methods used by industrialists to sell their products.

_____ **7.** Company towns built by George Pullman were compared to feudal estates.

■ REVIEWING FACTS Choose the correct items from the following list to complete the statements below.

department stores	Gospel of Wealth	John D. Rockefeller
railroad	Andrew Carnegie	large quantities
marketing	Sears, Roebuck, and Co.	vertical integration

1. According to the _____, gaining great wealth was a sign of God's blessing.

2. Although he was acquiring great wealth in the steel industry, _____ believed that the wealthy should give their wealth to society before their deaths.

3. Buying the company that supplied your company with raw materials and then buying the railway company that shipped your product would be an example of

_____.

4. Using one company to control other companies making the same product was a method

used by _____ to expand his business.

5. Cornelius Vanderbilt used his business skills to provide more efficient service in the

_____ industry.

6. Along with keeping the costs of making a product as low as possible and trying to control businesses that competed with them, industrialists also developed new ways of

_____ their product.

7. _____ was one of the largest companies in which a wide variety of things could be bought, paid for, and delivered by mail.

8. In addition to offering a wide variety of products in one location,

_____ also provided women with opportunities for work.

9. Buying _____ of goods allowed department and chain stores to sell at lower prices than smaller stores.

The Second Industrial Revolution

MAIN IDEA ACTIVITIES 6.3

■ VOCABULARY

Some expressions to understand:

- **wan-faced (209):** pale
- **militant existence (211):** a way of living that is like being in the military

Other terms:

- **tariff (209):** a special fee added to the price of goods imported from another country
- **textile (210):** cloth
- **canneries (211):** factories where food is processed and packed into sealed cans
- **fatigue (211):** a physical or mental feeling of being very tired

■ ORGANIZING INFORMATION Use the following items to complete the chart below comparing working conditions in the Second Industrial Revolution with those of today.

- ten- to twelve-hour workdays
- six- to seven-day workweeks
- company-paid health insurance
- no compensation for injury on the job
- safe working environment
- minorities paid less for the same job
- retirement plans
- paid vacations

Working Conditions

Second Industrial Age	Today
• _____	• _____
_____	_____
• _____	• _____
_____	_____
• _____	• _____
_____	_____
• _____	• _____
_____	_____

■ UNDERSTANDING MAIN IDEAS For each of the following, write the letter of the *best* choice in the space provided.

_____ 1. What law could not be enforced because the government did not clearly define monopolies and trusts?
   a. Homestead Act
   b. Federal Banking Act
   c. Sherman Antitrust Act
   d. Fourteenth Amendment

_____ 2. Which group of willing workers were prevented from working in southern textile mills?
   a. African Americans
   b. Norwegians
   c. Irish
   d. Italians

_____ 3. Because prices were higher at company stores, workers often had to spend their entire paychecks to buy
   a. automobiles.
   b. radios.
   c. food and clothing.
   d. nice furniture.

_____ 4. Who was the Irish American leader of the Knights of Labor who opened membership to women and unskilled workers?
   a. Uriah Stephens
   b. Terence V. Powderly
   c. John McCormick
   d. Samuel Gompers

_____ 5. People who were against her ideas called Mary Harris Jones
   a. "everyone's grandmother."
   b. "an overseer in a bonnet."
   c. "a man's worst nightmare."
   d. "the most dangerous woman in America."

_____ 6. One of the early strikes led by the Knights of Labor was against railroads owned by
   a. Jay Gould.
   b. John D. Rockefeller.
   c. George Westinghouse.
   d. Thomas Alva Edison.

_____ 7. The Haymarket Riot might have been avoided if workers had been successful in getting their request for
   a. a paid Christmas holiday.
   b. an eight-hour work day.
   c. a law stopping child labor.
   d. a company store.

_____ 8. To prevent a job applicant from joining a union, the employer would make him or her sign a
   a. yellow-dog contract.
   b. privacy agreement.
   c. blacklist.
   d. pay voucher.

_____ 9. African Americans sometimes acted as strikebreakers because they
   a. liked industry.
   b. believed in a good day's work.
   c. felt the unions had not helped them.
   d. were skilled tradesmen.

_____ 10. Who was the president who used federal troops to break a strike at a railroad sleeping-car factory?
   a. Grover Cleveland
   b. Ulysses S. Grant
   c. Rutherford B. Hayes
   d. John Adams

CHAPTER 7

The Transformation of American Society

MAIN IDEA ACTIVITIES 7.1

■ VOCABULARY

Some terms to understand:

- **commotion (220):** a lot of activity
- **hectic (220):** quick and excited movement
- **deported (221):** forced by a government order to leave a country
- **slums (222):** very poor and run-down parts of a city in which many people live
- **transition (223):** change to a new situation
- **bittersweet (224):** pleasant and unpleasant at the same time
- **motley throng (224):** a crowd of people that are very different from one another
- **rites (224):** rituals; ceremonies

■ ORGANIZING INFORMATION Complete the diagram below that compares the old immigrant population with the new immigrant population, using the following items.

- from northwestern Europe
- willing to endure many hardships
- Catholic, Greek Orthodox, or Jewish

- arrived in America from 1891 to 1910
- wanted to escape poverty
- Protestant

Old Immigrants
1. _____
2. _____

In Common
1. _____
2. _____

New Immigrants
1. _____
2. _____

■ EVALUATING INFORMATION Mark each statement *T* if it is true and *F* if it is false.

_____ **1.** In 1899 an emigrant from Greece would have been considered a new immigrant.

_____ **2.** Most new immigrants had left behind comfortable lives in northern Europe.

_____ **3.** Immigrants with physical diseases or without a way to support themselves were not allowed to enter the United States.

_____ **4.** Religious organizations often provided needy immigrants with food and clothing.

_____ **5.** Nativists believed that the new immigrants were good, hardworking people exactly like themselves.

_____ **6.** The Immigration Restriction League wanted to pass a law that all immigrants must be able to read before being allowed into the United States.

▩ REVIEWING FACTS Choose the correct items from the following list to complete the statements below.

citizens	industry	literacy tests
Statue of Liberty	steamship lines	benevolent societies
Workingmen's Party of California	Angel Island	jobs

1. The _____ would be one of the first things an immigrant coming to Ellis Island would see.

2. To try to persuade people to make a new home in the United States, some

   _____ offered low fares.

3. For many Asian immigrants, _____ in San Francisco Bay was their first experience with the United States.

4. Organizations that tried to help new immigrants find jobs or homes were called

   _____.

5. Nativists believed that because immigrants would work for very little money they would

   take away _____ that native-born Americans should have.

6. Even though it was led by an Irish immigrant, the _____ worked hard to stop Chinese immigrants from coming to the United States.

7. The Chinese Exclusion Act stated that Chinese immigrants could not become American

   _____.

8. President Grover Cleveland called a law requiring _____ for immigrants "illiberal, narrow, and un-American."

9. Without the contribution of immigrants, American _____ would not have been able to grow as fast as it did.

CHAPTER 7

The Transformation of American Society

MAIN IDEA ACTIVITIES 7.2

■ VOCABULARY

Some expressions to understand:

- **urban landscape** (226): the manner in which a city is designed
- **public transportation** (226): transportation systems used to move large numbers of people from place to place
- **fancy ball** (228): a party where people dress in very nice clothes
- **British Victorian culture** (228): a very conservative and structured view of life based on the ideals of Queen Victoria of Great Britain

Other terms:

- **etiquette** (228): rules that establish proper behavior
- **domain** (229): territory
- **clustered** (230): grouped together
- **crusades** (232): focused and controlled movements for or against a cause

■ EVALUATING INFORMATION Mark each statement *T* if it is true or *F* if it is false.

_____ **1.** The daily fares for commuter railroads were low enough that working-class and poor people could afford to live in the newly developed suburbs.

_____ **2.** Some of the people who had become rich during the late 1800s gave money to charities because it was a way to display their wealth publicly.

_____ **3.** Although there were more opportunities for women to work outside the home, upper-class women were still expected to limit their activities to home and family.

_____ **4.** Settlement houses were intended to help immigrants get to the new settlements in the western United States.

_____ **5.** Jane Addams believed that the college-educated women who volunteered at Hull House would learn about life from working with the working poor.

_____ **6.** The Social Gospel preached that people should spend more time enjoying conversations with each other in a social environment.

■ **UNDERSTANDING MAIN IDEAS** For each of the following, write the letter of the *best* choice in the space provided.

_____ 1. What invention made it practical to construct buildings with more than five stories?

a. 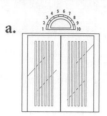   c.

b.    d.

_____ 2. Before the development of mass transit, most cities were no more than three square miles because
a. that was the distance a horse could gallop in one hour.
b. there were not enough people for a larger city.
c. that was the distance a person could walk in a few hours.
d. land outside of cities was needed for farming.

_____ 3. What U.S. city began to use electric streetcars as part of its mass transit system in 1887?
a. Chicago, Illinois
b. Washington, D.C.
c. New York City, New York
d. Richmond, Virginia

_____ 4. Carnegie, Rockefeller, Vanderbilt, and others who had made their fortunes in the new industries were members of a group called the
a. Wall Street Titans.
b. industry kings.
c. nouveau riche.
d. new immigrants.

_____ 5. *Godey's Lady's Book* and *The Ladies' Home Journal* are examples of magazines that tried to teach upper-class ladies how to be the ideal
a. professional woman.
b. Victorian woman.
c. social reformer.
d. teacher.

_____ 6. Growth in new industries and in cities resulted in an increased number of educated, middle-class
a. professionals.
b. children.
c. farmers.
d. athletes.

_____ 7. In 1900 nearly half the population of New York City lived in
a. mansions.
b. hotels.
c. company-owned houses.
d. tenement buildings.

_____ 8. Who in the city population was described by this statement: "They vote without fear . . ."?
a. southern whites
b. American Indians
c. African Americans
d. French Canadians

_____ 9. Who founded the People's Church?
a. Washington Gladden
b. Caroline Bartlett
c. Ward McAllister
d. Bradley Martin

_____ 10. The 1931 Nobel Peace Prize was given to
a. President Grover Cleveland.
b. Katherine Chorley.
c. Jane Addams.
d. Jay Gould.

The Transformation of American Society

MAIN IDEA ACTIVITIES 7.3

■ VOCABULARY

An expression to understand:

- **advice columns (235):** parts of newspapers where personal questions are asked and newspaper writers give suggestions

Other terms:

- **momentum (233):** energy; strength; force
- **sensational (235):** intended to cause a lot of curiosity or create a strong reaction
- **fancy illustrations (235):** pictures that use a lot of color or are in some other way able to catch your eye
- **entice (235):** to create a desire for something
- **refuge (236):** a shelter or place that provides protection
- **melodramatic (238):** exaggerates an emotion beyond what is realistic

■ EVALUATING INFORMATION Mark each statement *T* if it is true or *F* if it is false.

_____ 1. Social reformers saw education as one of the best ways to improve the lives of the urban working class.

_____ 2. In the new system, African Americans, Asian Americans, Hispanics, and whites all went to the same schools.

_____ 3. More people being able to read and the low cost of publishing encouraged the printing of many different types of newspapers.

_____ 4. Exciting stories, special features, and colorful cartoons were some of the things publishers tried in order to sell as many newspapers as possible.

_____ 5. During the late 1800s books about Christian principles sold more copies than any other type.

_____ 6. Abner Doubleday invented the game of baseball.

_____ 7. Baseball teams included both white and African American players.

_____ 8. In 1905, 18 college players and 46 high school players died in football games.

■ REVIEWING FACTS Choose the correct items from the list below to complete the following statements.

bicycling   Edwin Booth   dances
football   Edith Wharton   spectator sports
Cincinnati Red Stockings   vaudeville   John Dewey

1. A school science experiment was an example of _____'s belief that students learn more by doing than by merely listening to lectures and memorizing facts.

2. William Dean Howells and _____ were two authors who wrote books that tried to describe life as it really was.

3. _____ was an outdoor activity that both men and women enjoyed during the late 1800s.

4. The first professional baseball team was called the _____.

5. The game of _____ started out as a college game played at New England schools for the upper class.

6. Baseball, football, and basketball were called _____ because people could enjoy watching them as much as playing them.

7. Famous for plays like *Romeo and Juliet* and *Hamlet,* _____ was one of the most popular actors of the 1860s and 1870s.

8. _____ was a type of theater that might include dancing dogs in its acts.

9. The Cakewalk, the Grizzly Bear, and the Turkey Trot were all names of popular

_____.

■ ORGANIZING INFORMATION Complete the graphic organizer about the development of American sports in the late 1800s using the following items. You will use some items more than one time.

- women encouraged to play
- evolved from a British game
- had professional leagues

- many serious injuries during early years of play
- excluded African American players
- invented in the United States

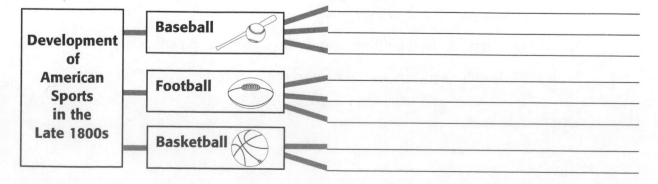

Politics in the Gilded Age

CHAPTER 8

MAIN IDEA ACTIVITIES 8.1

■ VOCABULARY

Some expressions to understand:

- **intoxicating drinks (248):** alcohol
- **comically exaggerated (250):** some feature or idea enlarged in an amusing way
- **tipped off (250):** being given information before it becomes known to others

Other terms:

- **sanitation (246):** cleaning up or removing waste materials
- **eligible (247):** qualified
- **constituents (247):** people who are part of a group that is represented by an elected official
- **indictment (251):** charging someone with committing a crime

■ ORGANIZING INFORMATION Complete the chart about political machines by listing their advantages and disadvantages.

Political Machines

Advantages	Disadvantages
• _____ _____ • _____ _____	• _____ _____ • _____ _____

██ **REVIEWING FACTS** **Choose the correct items from the following list to complete the statements below.**

voting fraud	immigrants	political machines
Irish Americans	Charles Tyson Yerkes	Jim Pendergast
public	cartoons	Tammany Hall

1. Trading votes for favors, jobs, and services were some of the ways that power remained in

   the hands of _____.

2. Because of the benefits political machines often provided to the poor,

   _____ were some of their biggest supporters.

3. _____ had a great advantage in becoming part of the political
   process because their native language was English.

4. Political machines hiring people to vote more than once while using different names is an

   example of _____.

5. Graft was a particularly harmful aspect of political machines because it often involved private individuals making a profit from money that belonged to the

   _____.

6. By bribing a Chicago alderman to support city laws that would benefit his street railway

   lines, _____ ended up with a very profitable monopoly in the
   public transportation system.

7. _____ was a Kansas City political boss who was very well liked
   because of his generosity toward the various immigrants that lived in his district.

8. William Marcy Tweed developed one of the most powerful political machines of the 1800s,

   _____, in New York; but it was destroyed when public opinion
   turned against him.

9. Thomas Nast's talent for creating humorous _____ did a great
   deal to destroy William Marcy Tweed's political machine.

Politics in the Gilded Age

MAIN IDEA ACTIVITIES 8.2

■ VOCABULARY

Some expressions to understand:

• **spoils system (253):** a system in which benefits or profits from an action are shared by one's friends or business partners

• **nail in a coffin (253):** action that contributes to the destruction or death of something or someone

• **according to its lights (254):** in agreement with its perspective

• **mudslinging (257):** making statements that are intended to expose a political opponent as not being trustworthy

Other terms:

• **barren (252):** empty

• **looted (252):** stole

• **tarnished (253):** lost its shine, like the surface of silver will dull over time

• **boss (254):** be the leader or have the authority

■ ORGANIZING INFORMATION Complete the graphic organizer about the struggle for honest government by placing the following events in chronological order.

• Liberal Republican Party was formed
• Whiskey Ring scandal
• Stalwarts and Half-Breeds split Republicans
• Republican Congress weakened civil service reform movement
• Pendleton Civil Service Act passed
• President Garfield assassinated

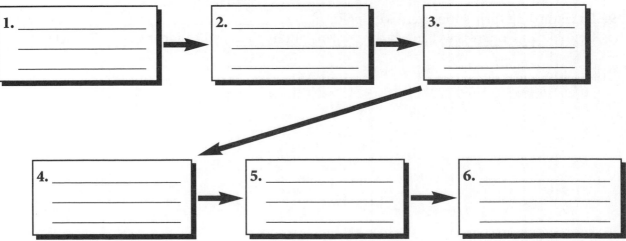

The Struggle for Honest Government

1. _____
2. _____
3. _____
4. _____
5. _____
6. _____

■ **REVIEWING FACTS** **Choose the correct items from the following list to complete the statements below.**

Liberal Republican Party	Mark Twain	Pendleton Civil Service Act
merit	Chester A. Arthur	gold
Stalwarts	an honest man	Benjamin Harrison

1. The attempts of Jay Gould and Abel Rathbone Corbin to make a quick and large profit in the buying and selling of _____ was the cause of one of the early scandals of Grant's presidency.

2. The _____ was formed as a response to the scandals during President Grant's administration.

3. The period of history called the Gilded Age got its name from a satirical novel written by Charles Dudley Warner and _____.

4. The part of the Republican Party that was against civil service reform was called the _____.

5. Julius Bing was one of the first of the Half-Breeds to support the idea of granting civil service jobs based on _____ instead of political patronage.

6. Republican presidential candidate James A. Garfield supported reform; but his running mate, _____, did not support reform.

7. Even though it concerned only about 10 percent of federal jobs, the _____ was one of the first steps toward laws that awarded federal jobs based on merit instead of patronage.

8. The New York *World* defended Democratic presidential candidate Grover Cleveland from the mudslingers by calling him _____.

9. By rewarding their supporters with political jobs, _____ and the Republican Congress weakened the reforms put in place by President Grover Cleveland.

CHAPTER 8

Politics in the Gilded Age

MAIN IDEA ACTIVITIES 8.3

▮▮ VOCABULARY

Some expressions to understand:

- **tenant farmers (259):** farmers who live on and work land but do not own it
- **in good faith (259):** according to the belief that what you have been told is truthful
- **loan shark (261):** a person who lends money at extremely high interest rates, often with the support of a criminal organization

Other terms:

- **merged (260):** joined together
- **coalition (261):** an alliance
- **redeemable (262):** able to be exchanged for something of value
- **grassroots (263):** local
- **triggered (263):** started
- **predominantly (264):** for the most part

▮▮ CLASSIFYING INFORMATION Complete the graphic organizer about characteristics of the National Grange and the National Farmers' Alliance, using the following items.

- formed cooperatives to help members
- active with railroad freight rates
- wanted the silver standard
- supported the Populist Party

- worked for a graduated income tax
- fought for tougher bank regulations
- first major farmers' organization

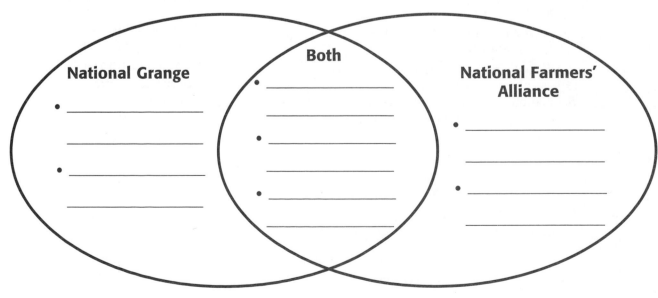

▥ UNDERSTANDING MAIN IDEAS For each of the following, write the letter of the *best* choice in the space provided.

_____ 1. What were farmers often forced to use as security for their loans?
   a. cattle
   b. their farms
   c. portion of their crops
   d. savings accounts

_____ 2. Who started the National Grange as a social organization for farmers?
   a. Grover Cleveland
   b. R. M. Humphrey
   c. Oliver Hudson Kelley
   d. William Jennings Bryan

_____ 3. One reason the Alliance was not able to combine its leadership was because of racial issues between the Southern Alliance and the
   a. National Grange.
   b. Interstate Commerce Commission.
   c. northern industries.
   d. Colored Farmers' Alliance.

_____ 4. With the gold standard, the amount of paper money in circulation was limited by
   a. the amount of gold in the U.S. Treasury.
   b. the number of silver mines.
   c. the number of gold coins in circulation.
   d. the silver standard.

_____ 5. Which was one of the laws that required the government to buy silver and mint coins on a monthly basis?
   a. Interstate Commerce Act
   b. Bland-Allison Act
   c. Income Tax Act
   d. Federal Antitrust Act

_____ 6. The Populist Party platform wanted restrictions on
   a. mining companies.
   b. voting rights.
   c. terms of office.
   d. immigration.

_____ 7. What law did President Grover Cleveland blame for the economic depression of 1893?
   a. Sherman Silver Purchase Act
   b. Interstate Commerce Act
   c. Farmers' Alliance Act
   d. State Railway Act

_____ 8. William Jennings Bryan gave his famous "Cross of Gold" speech in support of
   a. the gold standard.
   b. paper money.
   c. the silver standard.
   d. the Republican Party.

_____ 9. Although the Populist Party did much good for farmers, it did not seem to offer enough benefit to
   a. urban workers.
   b. the National Grange.
   c. the Farmers' Alliance.
   d. southern white farmers.

_____ 10. Eventually known for his influence over Congress, who won the presidential election of 1896?
   a. Grover Cleveland
   b. Chester Arthur
   c. William McKinley
   d. William Jennings Bryan

CHAPTER
9

The Age of Reform

MAIN IDEA ACTIVITIES 9.1

■ VOCABULARY

Some terms to understand:

• **tramp (274):** a person who travels around without purpose; a beggar

• **subsidiary (275):** secondary in importance

• **endeavoring (275):** doing something with a conscious effort to achieve a goal

• **curriculum (276):** course of study offered by a school

• **loaded dice (277):** dice that have been weighted to land with certain numbers facing up

• **intellectuals (279):** people who take a rational rather than emotional perspective toward an issue

■ ORGANIZING INFORMATION Complete the chart about actions taken in the Age of Reform, using the following items.

• end child labor
• public education

• election reforms
• minimum wage

• greater control in all areas of government
• journalism that exposed harmful social issues

Action in the Age of Reform

Business	• _____ _____	• _____ _____
Social Justice	• _____ _____	• _____ _____
Democracy	• _____ _____	• _____ _____

■ REVIEWING FACTS Choose the correct items from the following list to complete the statements below.

middle class	women	social reform
Social Gospel	progressivism	Herbert Croly
muckrakers	John D. Rockefeller	lynching

1. Unlike populism, which focused on the needs of farmers, _____ concentrated on the needs of people living in cities.

2. Men and women from the _____ were particularly attracted to the ideals of progressivism.

3. Because the culture of the time limited their career options, many

   _____ turned to reform efforts as a way to use knowledge they had gained in college.

4. The book *What Eight Million Women Want* pointed out the special role of women in

   efforts toward _____.

5. Progressives and believers in the _____ philosophy often shared the same ideals for society.

6. Ida Tarbell was known as the "Terror of the Trusts" because of a series of articles she wrote

   about the business practices of _____.

7. To Ray Stannard Baker, one of the most horrible things about the

   _____ he witnessed in Springfield, Ohio, was the lack of concern shown by the public.

8. Journalists and authors who wrote stories exposing corruption or other social problems

   were often called _____.

9. The concept that government should use its regulatory and tax powers to help all citizens

   was the idea of a progressive intellectual named _____.

CHAPTER 9

The Age of Reform

MAIN IDEA ACTIVITIES 9.2

■ VOCABULARY

Some terms to understand:

- **meager (280):** lacking in quantity; a small amount
- **cave-ins (280):** tunnels collapsing, roofs falling in
- **stifled (280):** interrupted or silenced
- **pieceworkers (280):** workers who are paid by the number of pieces they finish
- **steel hoppers (281):** funnel-shaped containers in which things may be stored
- **highlighted (282):** centered attention on
- **boycotts (285):** agreements made by groups of people not to purchase a product or service as a means of protesting

■ ORGANIZING INFORMATION Complete the chart of characteristics of the three major unions, using the following items.

- members from minority races
- skilled workers only
- against capitalism
- major labor organization of the time
- received strike support from Women's Trade Union League
- mainly Jewish and Italian immigrant women

Characteristics of Major Unions

AFL	• _____	• _____
ILGWU	• _____	• _____
IWW	• _____	• _____

■ **EVALUATING INFORMATION** Mark each statement *T* if it is true or *F* if it is false.

_____ **1.** In the book *The Bitter Cry of the Children,* John Spargo compared child labor practices to slavery.

_____ **2.** Many employers simply ignored child labor laws limiting the number of hours a child could work.

_____ **3.** The Supreme Court always supported social reform.

_____ **4.** The encouragement of racist policies was one of the effects of the American Federation of Labor's refusal to admit unskilled workers as members.

■ **REVIEWING FACTS** Choose the correct items from the following list to complete the statements below.

fire-safety
socialism
Industrial Workers of the World
Brandeis Brief
Fourteenth Amendment
closed shop
Commission on Industrial Relations
International Ladies' Garment Workers Union
National Child Labor Committee

1. Child labor practices and the low wages women earned were two labor issues attacked by the

_____.

2. As organizer of the _____, Florence Kelley was very effective in persuading state legislatures to pass laws that prohibited companies from hiring young children.

3. The New York legislature passed the nation's strictest _____ code as a result of the tragedy at the Triangle Shirtwaist Company.

4. In an attempt to uphold an Oregon law limiting the number of hours a woman could work,

lawyer Louis Brandeis developed the _____.

5. Factory owners cited the _____ to argue against new laws that regulated their businesses.

6. One of the biggest goals for the newly developing labor unions was the

_____ workplace, where all employees must belong to a union.

7. Some unions favored an economic system called _____, where most factories and other public service functions would be owned by the government or worker cooperatives.

8. The "Uprising of 20,000" strike was an attempt by thousands of workers to force their

companies to recognize the _____ as their union.

9. _____ was the only labor union of the time that actively sought out African American, Asian American, and Hispanic workers to become members.

The Age of Reform

CHAPTER 9

MAIN IDEA ACTIVITIES 9.3

■ VOCABULARY

Some expressions to understand:

- **pandemonium reigned** (287): everything was noisy and disorganized
- **grandfather clause** (291): the terms of a law do not apply if a situation existed before the law was passed

Other terms:

- **referendum** (287): call for a direct vote by the people
- **shunned** (287): avoided
- **arch enemy** (288): a particularly bad opponent
- **evangelist** (289): a Protestant preacher
- **steamy** (289): erotic

■ EVALUATING INFORMATION Mark each statement *T* if it is true or *F* if it is false.

_____ **1.** Social reformers did not consider tenement housing or sanitation issues important enough problems to require their attention.

_____ **2.** Daniel Burnham believed that good city planning was the responsibility of city government.

_____ **3.** George Kibbe Turner wrote that saloons were harmless places for the lower classes to meet and enjoy conversation.

_____ **4.** Nickelodeons were movie houses where admission tickets cost 5 or 10 cents.

_____ **5.** In the civil rights case *Buchanan* v. *Warley,* the Supreme Court ruled that Kentucky could not require separate housing for whites and nonwhites.

_____ **6.** Madison Grant was a social progressive who held racist opinions about African Americans, Jews, and immigrants from certain parts of Europe.

■ UNDERSTANDING MAIN IDEAS For each of the following, write the letter of the *best* choice in the space provided.

_____ 1. Who was the settlement-house worker who became very active in trying to reform conditions in tenement housing?
   a. Louise DeKoven Bowen
   b. Daniel Burnham
   c. Frederic Howe
   d. Lawrence Veiller

_____ 2. According to the New York State Tenement House Commission, which state had the most serious tenement house problem in the world?
   a. California
   b. New York
   c. Illinois
   d. New Jersey

_____ 3. Who described his personal experiences with the stench, dirt, and noise of tenement buildings?
   a. Henry Moscowitz
   b. Lawrence Veiller
   c. Daniel Burnham
   d. William Dean Howells

_____ 4. Which amendment barred the manufacture, sale, and distribution of alcoholic beverages in the United States?
   a. Fourteenth Amendment
   b. Fifteenth Amendment
   c. Eighteenth Amendment
   d. Seventeenth Amendment

_____ 5. Who believed that movies would lure people to become evil?
   a. William Dean Howells
   b. Henry Moscowitz
   c. Frances Willard
   d. Senator William Kenyon

_____ 6. The National Association for the Advancement of Colored People was the direct result of a joint effort between W. E. B. Du Bois and
   a. American Indians.
   b. southern farmers.
   c. white progressives.
   d. Asian Americans.

■ INTERPRETING VISUAL IMAGES Examine the drawings and answer the question that follows.

New York State Tenement House Bill

Before

After

What are two obvious changes in the buildings that were a direct result of the passage of the New York State Tenement House Bill?

• _____

• _____

CHAPTER 10 Progressive Politicians

MAIN IDEA ACTIVITIES 10.1

VOCABULARY

Some terms to understand:

- **martyrdom (298):** sacrificing or suffering a great deal in order to further a cause or belief
- **depicted (298):** used a picture or words to represent an idea
- **documenting (298):** writing or a photograph that serves as proof that something was said or done
- **coercion (299):** a force or threat
- **overhauled (300):** something that has been closely examined and repaired
- **hindered (300):** delayed progress

CLASSIFYING INFORMATION Complete the graphic organizer about voting reform by listing the items below under the correct example.

- recall
- referendum
- initiative

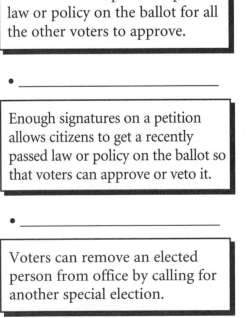
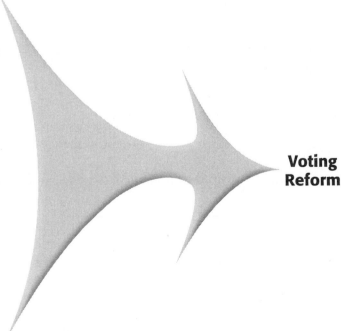

Voters have the power to put a law or policy on the ballot for all the other voters to approve.

• _____

Enough signatures on a petition allows citizens to get a recently passed law or policy on the ballot so that voters can approve or veto it.

• _____

Voters can remove an elected person from office by calling for another special election.

• _____

Voting Reform

■ REVIEWING FACTS Choose the correct items from the following list to complete the statements below.

voter	election process	Robert M. La Follette
U.S. Senate	secret ballot	Wisconsin Idea
direct primary	city manager	African Americans
city commission	lower classes	Samuel M. "Golden Rule" Jones

1. Because they traded tax breaks and favors for large donations of money to their election

    campaigns, the _____ was sometimes referred to as the
    Millionaire's Club.

2. Progressives believed that the best way to break the power of political machines was to

    reform the _____.

3. A political event where voters choose the candidates who will later run in a general election

    is called a _____.

4. The _____ proved to be very effective in preventing voters from
    being threatened or forced to vote for one candidate or another.

5. Because he believed that the principle of "Do unto others as you would have them do unto
    you" should be applied to city government, the mayor of Toledo, Ohio, in 1897 was called

    _____.

6. Tax reform and pensions for city employees are two examples of progressive reform efforts

    that were rejected by the average _____.

7. Electoral reform was hurt by the belief of some middle-class progressives that the

    _____ might have too much power in the election process.

8. A state-appointed group of experts who were not party loyalists made up the first

    _____ that was so helpful in Galveston, Texas, after a hurricane in 1900.

9. A person who was hired to manage a city the same way he or she would manage a business

    was called a _____.

10. The _____ was a model reform program that introduced the
    direct primary and other electoral changes to Wisconsin and other states.

11. Even though they did much for poor whites, the southern progressives still tried to prevent

    _____ from voting.

12. _____ was the Wisconsin governor who was responsible for
    actively supporting electoral reforms in his state.

Progressive Politicians

CHAPTER 10

MAIN IDEA ACTIVITIES 10.2

▉ VOCABULARY

Some expressions to understand:

- **bully pulpit (303):** a good position from which to make known views or to rally support for a particular cause
- **square deal (304):** something that is fair for everyone concerned

Other terms:

- **anarchist (303):** person who rebels against any authority or ruling power
- **impulsive (304):** acting quickly on something that is felt rather than first thinking it out
- **impotent (305):** not having strength or power
- **opiates (306):** drugs that cause sleepiness or deaden the senses
- **mesh (307):** something that catches people or things, as in a net
- **indissolubly (307):** something that is permanent or cannot be dissolved
- **enduring (308):** lasting for a long time

▉ EVALUATING INFORMATION Mark each statement *T* if it is true and *F* if it is false.

_____ **1.** President Roosevelt was a "hands-off" president, preferring not to become too closely involved with important issues that might cost him votes.

_____ **2.** The "bully pulpit" refers to a special kind of speaker's stand that President Roosevelt's minister used during religious services.

_____ **3.** Instead of sending in federal troops to break up the United Mine Workers' strike, Roosevelt appointed a commission of arbitrators to look at the situation.

_____ **4.** Roosevelt was very much against business and the wealth that it created for its owners.

_____ **5.** In the early 1900s, some food processors fooled the consumer by churning spoiled butter with skim milk so that they could sell the butter as fresh.

_____ **6.** Because they were the people who most often bought food, women became very involved in the food reform movement.

■ UNDERSTANDING MAIN IDEAS For each of the following, write the letter of the *best* choice in the space provided.

_____ 1. Who was the reform minister who first asked President Roosevelt for help during the United Mine Workers' strike?
   a. Mark Hanna
   b. James J. Hill
   c. Washington Gladden
   d. Upton Sinclair

_____ 2. In whose favor did the arbitrators finally decide in the UMW strike?
   a. both miners and owners
   b. miners
   c. owners
   d. President Roosevelt

_____ 3. President Roosevelt's efforts to balance the needs of business, consumers, and labor was called the
   a. bully pulpit.
   b. Square Deal.
   c. One Strike Idea.
   d. Pan-American Exposition.

_____ 4. The Roosevelt administration's victory in its lawsuit against the Northern Securities Company launched which government campaign?
   a. trustbusting
   b. moneybreaking
   c. favor lending
   d. labor loving

_____ 5. The Elkins Act was intended to stop what type of companies from accepting rebates from their customers?

_____ 6. Mrs. Winslow's Soothing Syrup for teething babies was the same medicine that the British had labeled
   a. tea.
   b. sugar water.
   c. baking soda.
   d. poison.

_____ 7. The novel *The Jungle* was about unsanitary conditions in
   a. railroad cars.
   b. meatpacking plants.
   c. tenement buildings.
   d. bakeries.

_____ 8. The Pure Food and Drug Act was one of the laws enacted in response to a report written by Secretary of Agriculture
   a. Theodore Roosevelt.
   b. Edward Bok.
   c. E. H. Harriman.
   d. James Wilson.

_____ 9. Which Roosevelt supporter first used the word *conservation* to describe responsible protection of the natural environment?
   a. Gifford Pinchot
   b. William Jennings Bryan
   c. Leon Czolgosz
   d. Judge Alton Parker

_____ 10. One lasting gift to the nation from the Roosevelt administration was more
   a. railroad lines.
   b. public transportation.
   c. steady jobs.
   d. national parks.

CHAPTER
10

Progressive Politicians

MAIN IDEA ACTIVITIES 10.3

■ VOCABULARY

An expression to understand:

• **deepened the gulf (312):** made them even further apart in their views

Other terms:

• **safari (310):** a journey or a trip, usually hunting

• **stances (310):** positions

• **sabotaging (311):** a deliberate attempt to ruin the progress of a cause or activity

• **paramount (311):** of the highest importance

• **bracketed (311):** something came before and after it

■ ORGANIZING INFORMATION Complete the chart about the political positions of Taft and the Progressive Party, using the items below.

• expand presidential power
• presidential power limited by Constitution
• supported Gifford Pinchot

• did not oppose high tariffs
• wanted low tariffs
• supported Richard Ballinger

Taft   *Progressive Party*

• _____   • _____

   _____   _____

• _____   • _____

   _____   _____

• _____   • _____

   _____   _____

REVIEWING FACTS Choose the correct items from the following list to complete the statements below.

Mann-Elkins Act	Theodore Roosevelt	Payne-Aldrich Tariff
Woodrow Wilson	New Freedom	New Nationalism
Bull Moose Party	conservation	Joseph "Uncle Joe" Cannon

1. The _____, which gave power to the Interstate Commerce Commission to regulate telephone and telegraph companies, was enacted during Taft's term of office.

2. One of the first steps leading to the split between President Taft and the Republican progressives was his refusal to veto the _____ Bill.

3. The conflict between Gifford Pinchot and Richard Ballinger over the sale of public lands was viewed by progressive Republicans as an attempt to overturn Roosevelt's

_____ program.

4. Former president Roosevelt's _____ program called for an active federal government to pass laws protecting people and regulating business.

5. Progressive Republicans believed that Speaker of the House _____ had too much control over which bills reached the House floor for debate.

6. Because Taft's allies would not seat many of Roosevelt's delegates,

_____ lost the Republican Party's 1912 presidential nomination.

7. The newly formed Progressive Party was also known as the _____.

8. The split in the Republican Party resulted in Democrats and some conservative Republicans

supporting _____ for president.

9. The _____ program introduced by President Wilson was built on his belief that people did best with the least amount of interference from government and business.

Progressive Politicians

MAIN IDEA ACTIVITIES 10.4

■ VOCABULARY

An expression to understand:

• **dishonorable discharge (320):** being released from the armed forces for a serious offense

Other terms:

• **muster (315):** to cause things to come together
• **superstitious (316):** someone who believes that one thing influences the outcome of another even though there is no logical connection between the two
• **hamper (316):** get in the way of something
• **degenerated (317):** fell apart
• **plaintive (317):** sorrowful or sad
• **anemic (317):** weak
• **raved (318):** spoke about it with a lot of excitement

■ ORGANIZING INFORMATION Complete the chart about legislation during the Wilson administration by matching the following items with the appropriate drawings.

• Federal Reserve Act
• Federal Workmen's Compensation Act
• Nineteenth Amendment
• Federal Farm Loan Act
• Clayton Antitrust Act

Legislation During the Wilson Administration

(building)	• _____
(person in bed)	• _____
(VOTE)	• _____
(tractor)	• _____
(factory)	• _____

■ REVIEWING FACTS Choose the correct items from the following list to complete the statements below.

African Americans   graduated income tax
Carrie Chapman Catt   National American Woman Suffrage Association
child labor   Federal Trade Commission
National Woman's Party

1. To make up for revenue lost by lowering tariffs, Wilson's administration introduced the

    _____.

2. The creation of the _____ gave the government the ability to
   investigate and bring to court corporations that had unfair business practices.

3. Even though he had many successes in different areas, Wilson was unable to achieve lasting

    reform in the area of _____.

4. The _____ tried to get voting rights for women by changing laws
   at the state level.

5. The _____, founded by Alice Paul, wanted to have an amendment
   to the Constitution guaranteeing women the right to vote.

6. As a teacher, writer, and voting rights activist, _____ 's winning
   plan eventually led to successes at the state level for women's suffrage.

7. Even though they were considered progressive presidents, Woodrow Wilson and Teddy
   Roosevelt did not push for a change in laws that would help

    _____.

America and the World

MAIN IDEA ACTIVITIES 11.1

■ VOCABULARY

Some expressions to understand:

- **faced off (326):** confronted each other with determination
- **coaling station (327):** a port or place where steamships could load coal for fuel
- **laid siege (330):** surrounded for a long time

Other terms:

- **quest (326):** a search
- **brink (326):** the edge of something
- **impelled (329):** driven forward
- **handbills (330):** printed sheets of paper that are given out by hand
- **crucial (332):** important
- **dazzling (332):** amazing

■ ORGANIZING INFORMATION Complete the graphic organizer about the reasons for imperialism by placing an *X* next to the views each person held.

Reasons for Imperialism

	Henry Cabot Lodge	Alfred Thayer Mahan	Josiah Strong
Economic and Military Security			
Strong Naval Presence			
Civilization and Christianity			

▓ EVALUATING INFORMATION Mark each statement *T* if it is true and *F* if it is false.

_____ **1.** Thousands of native Hawaiians died from diseases brought by missionaries, settlers, and traders.

_____ **2.** The Hawaiian League was a secret organization whose goal was to overthrow the Hawaiian monarchy and persuade the United States to annex Hawaii.

_____ **3.** The Bayonet Constitution refers to an agreement between the Hawaiian monarchy and the United States that the use of bayonets on the Hawaiian Islands would be illegal.

_____ **4.** Queen Liliuokalani believed that being annexed by the United States was in the best interests of the Hawaiian people.

_____ **5.** Most of the people of Hawaii did not want the United States to annex their islands.

_____ **6.** The Open Door Policy refers to an agreement that China would allow all nations the same amount of access to trade and investments.

_____ **7.** The Fists of Righteous Harmony was another name for the secret Chinese society called the Boxers.

_____ **8.** The Boxer Rebellion was the result of Chinese resentment toward the presence of foreigners in China.

_____ **9.** The Russo-Japanese War began when the United States sent Commodore Matthew Perry to Japan.

_____ **10.** President Theodore Roosevelt was awarded the Nobel Peace Prize in 1905 because of his role in negotiating peace between Russia and Japan.

CHAPTER 11 — America and the World

MAIN IDEA ACTIVITIES 11.2

▇ VOCABULARY

Some expressions to understand:

• **trained his eyes (335):** focused his eyes

• **provisional government (339):** a temporary government

Other terms:

• **simmered (333):** filled with emotion that is being pushed down or controlled

• **atrocities (334):** horrible acts of cruelty and violence

• **artifacts (334):** ornaments of artistic or historic interest

• **intercepted (335):** interrupted the progress

• **picket (337):** a group of aircraft, soldiers, or weapons that warns of an enemy's approach

• **travail (337):** very hard or painful work

▇ EVALUATING INFORMATION Mark each statement *T* if it is true and *F* if it is false.

_____ **1.** José Martí was a Cuban exile living in New York who took up the cause of Cuban independence.

_____ **2.** To many Americans, the Cubans' struggle for independence reminded them of the American fight for independence against the British.

_____ **3.** William Randolph Hearst believed that newspapers were extremely powerful because they were the voice of the federal government.

_____ **4.** Because of his experiences in the Civil War, President William McKinley was against any American action in support of the Cuban rebels.

_____ **5.** The Philippine Islands were American territories in the Pacific that the government of Spain attempted to steal away.

_____ **6.** Emilio Aguinaldo was a famous Cuban rebel who died during the fighting with Spain.

▥ UNDERSTANDING MAIN IDEAS For each of the following, write the letter of the *best* choice in the space provided.

_____ **1.** Which Spanish general was called the Butcher by the American press because of his cruel treatment of Cubans?
a. Francisco Franco
b. Valeriano Weyler
c. José Martí
d. Emilio Aguinaldo

_____ **2.** The tragedy that was the final push toward war with Spain was the explosion of the

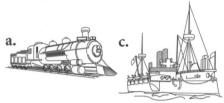

_____ **3.** Who was the naval officer who was ordered by Secretary of the Navy Theodore Roosevelt to attack the Philippines?
a. Commodore George Dewey
b. Admiral Horatio Nelson
c. Commodore Richard Perry
d. Admiral John Newhouse

_____ **4.** Who was one of the most powerful journalists of the time who believed that newspapers as the voice of the people could control the nation?
a. George Pulitzer
b. William Randolph Hearst
c. Henry Cabot Lodge
d. William Jennings Bryan

_____ **5.** The cavalry unit made up of American Indians, college athletes, cowboys, and ranchers that was led by Theodore Roosevelt was called the
a. Rough Riders.
b. Saviors of Santiago.
c. Martí Brigade.
d. San Juan Heroes.

_____ **6.** Opponents of the United States annexation of the Philippines believed that to do so would be a violation of the
a. U.S. Constitution.
b. Fourteenth Amendment.
c. Emancipation Proclamation.
d. Declaration of Independence.

_____ **7.** Many people in favor of annexation agreed with former minister to China Charles Denby when he said,
a. "Sink the Bismarck!"
b. "It's our duty!"
c. "Commerce, not politics, is king."
d. "Save Sergeant Crittendon."

_____ **8.** Establishing a governor and a two-house legislature, the Philippine Government Act was also known as the
a. Spanish-American War Act.
b. Emilio Aguinaldo Act.
c. Manila Act.
d. Organic Act.

CHAPTER
11

America and the World

MAIN IDEA ACTIVITIES 11.3

■ VOCABULARY

An expression to understand:

• **a near standstill (342):** situation in which nearly all activity has stopped

Other terms:

• **sovereignty (341):** the supreme authority or power

• **avalanche (342):** a large amount of falling or sliding earth or snow

■ ORGANIZING INFORMATION Complete the chart about the use of the Monroe Doctrine, using the following items.

• Haiti
• Nicaragua

• dollar diplomacy
• democratic government

• Dominican Republic
• Roosevelt Corollary

Use of the Monroe Doctrine

President	Policy	Place
Theodore Roosevelt		
William Howard Taft		
Woodrow Wilson		

▨ REVIEWING FACTS Choose the correct items from the following list to complete the statements below.

Panama	Cuba	yellow fever
Hemisphere	Philippe Bunau-Varilla	Puerto Rico
John Hay	Path Between the Seas	Theodore Roosevelt

1. Once _____ agreed to the Platt Amendment, it became a protec-torate of the United States.

2. The Foraker Act and the Jones Act were two steps the United States took in the process of

   making _____ a self-governing commonwealth.

3. Although the French had tried to build a canal in Panama, the United States started its

   efforts when Secretary of State _____ began negotiations with Colombia.

4. _____ was the engineer for the French Panama Canal project who helped the Panamanian rebels get support from the United States.

5. Army colonel Dr. William C. Gorgas applied his experiences with tropical diseases in Cuba

   to improving health conditions in _____.

6. Carried by mosquitoes, _____ was one of the most serious causes of disease for those working on the canal.

7. The Panama Canal was also called the _____.

8. The West African proverb that began "Walk softly and carry a big stick" was a favorite of

   _____.

9. Presidents Taft, Wilson, and Roosevelt all believed that the United States was the protector

   of the Western _____.

America and the World

MAIN IDEA ACTIVITIES 11.4

▮▮ VOCABULARY

An expression to understand:

• **national will (345):** the wishes of the people

Other terms:

• **tyranny (345):** a situation in which one person has total authority over everyone else and uses the power unfairly or cruelly

• **toppled (346):** pushed over or brought down

• **hoist (347):** raise

• **bombardment (347):** an attack with bombs or shells

• **disbanded (348):** broke up; dissolved

• **eluded (349):** avoided

▮▮ ORGANIZING INFORMATION Complete the graphic organizer by placing the following events in chronological order.

• Porfirio Díaz takes power
• Pancho Villa attacks Columbus, New Mexico
• Victoriano Huerta seizes control
• General Pershing arrives in Mexico
• new Mexican constitution created

• Zapata rebels
• Francisco Madero wins elections
• U.S. troops withdrawn
• Venustiano Carranza takes power
• U.S. troops in Veracruz

1. _____

2. _____

3. _____

4. _____

5. _____

6. _____

7. _____

8. _____

9. _____

10. _____

■ **EVALUATING INFORMATION** Mark each statement *T* if it is true and *F* if it is false.

_____ **1.** Porfirio Díaz was directly responsible for improvements in the mining, petroleum, and railroad industries.

_____ **2.** Emiliano Zapata led a rebel army that fought for land for Indian peasants.

_____ **3.** Even though he came from the upper classes, the ideas of Francisco Madero were used to rebel against Venustiano Carranza.

_____ **4.** Because they all wanted the same thing, the rebel leaders were able to group together and fight as one force.

_____ **5.** Pancho Villa, Álvaro Obregón, Emiliano Zapata, and Venustiano Carranza all were Mexican rebel leaders.

_____ **6.** Argentina, Brazil, and Chile were called the "ABC powers."

_____ **7.** Along with the European nations, President Woodrow Wilson recognized the government of Victoriano Huerta.

_____ **8.** Veracruz was the site of the first armed fight between the United States military and Mexican soldiers.

_____ **9.** General John J. Pershing was sent into Mexico to find Álvaro Obregón.

_____ **10.** Upset because the United States recognized Venustiano Carranza's government, Pancho Villa attacked Columbus, New Mexico.

_____ **11.** Venustiano Carranza's constitution gave all mineral, oil, and water rights to American businesses.

_____ **12.** Carranza's new constitution also provided protection for workers, such as the eight-hour workday and the abolition of child labor.

CHAPTER 12

World War I

MAIN IDEA ACTIVITIES 12.1

◼ VOCABULARY

An expression to understand:

• **unsustainable casualties (358):** more injuries to the fighting force than can be replaced

Other terms:

• **imminent (356):** about to happen
• **armaments (356):** weapons
• **ethnic groups (356):** people joined through language, national, racial, or religious background
• **disintegrate (357):** break apart into small pieces
• **hail (358):** so many bullets in the air it was like hail falling from the sky during a storm
• **stalemate (358):** a situation in which any further action is blocked

◼ EVALUATING INFORMATION Mark each statement *T* if it is true and *F* if it is false.

_____ **1.** The fact that European nations were formed based on the cultural heritage of their people contributed to an intense nationalism.

_____ **2.** Austria, Germany, and Italy formed one alliance, while France, Great Britain, and Russia formed another.

_____ **3.** At the beginning of the war, leaders believed that the fight would be short with a quick decision.

_____ **4.** To Germany's surprise, Belgium put up more of a resistance to the German advance than expected.

_____ **5.** The battle of Verdun was the longest of the war, with almost 1 million Allied Powers and Central Powers casualties.

_____ **6.** Disease and sickness in the trenches killed almost as many soldiers as combat did.

■ **REVIEWING FACTS** Choose the correct items from the following list to complete the statements below.

Archduke Franz Ferdinand	powder keg	Battle of the Somme
trench warfare	militarism	Allied Powers
Central Powers	Schlieffen Plan	

1. The Balkans were called the _____ of Europe because it was an area that seemed ready to erupt into violence.

2. The efforts of the major European nations to develop more powerful armies and weapons

   was a sign of the serious _____ that existed in Europe before the First World War.

3. The assassination of _____ by a Serbian nationalist caused Austria-Hungary to declare war on Serbia.

4. The alliance of Britain, France, and Russia was called the _____.

5. At first, the _____ was formed by an alliance between Austria-Hungary, Bulgaria, Germany, and the Ottoman Empire.

6. The _____ laid out the intention of Germany to invade Europe through Belgium and France thereby isolating Britain.

7. An artillery barrage followed by soldiers charging across open land were two characteristics

   of _____.

8. The _____ was an attempt by the Allied Powers to cause more casualties for the Germans than they could recover from.

■ **INTERPRETING VISUAL IMAGES** Examine the drawings below and answer the questions that follow.

poison gas   **barbed wire**   **tank**   **plane**

1. What are two examples of new weapons that were first used in World War I?

   _____

2. What product was found throughout no-man's-land? _____

3. Which of the weapons was silent? _____

World War I

CHAPTER
12

MAIN IDEA ACTIVITIES 12.2

▌ VOCABULARY

An expression to understand:

• **a lark (361):** an action that is done for fun

Other terms:

• **impartial (361):** not having an opinion that supports one side or the other

• **brutal (361):** violent; harsh

• **ultimatum (362):** a final statement that implies a punishment if it is not accepted

• **wanton (364):** needlessly cruel or merciless

• **wholesale (364):** complete

• **rain poncho (365):** a blanketlike coat with a hood that has a hole cut in the center for the head

• **drilling (365):** practicing the same movements or actions over and over again

▌ ORGANIZING INFORMATION Complete the chart below about the United States's policy of neutrality.

U.S. Neutrality

Wilson's Policy

He urged Americans to be neutral _____

Britain's Actions

Blockaded _____

Laid mines _____

Stopped U.S. ships _____

Germany's Actions

Established a war zone _____

Said ships entering it _____

March 28, 1915 _____

May 7, 1915 _____

American Reaction

Congress in June 1916 _____

■ **UNDERSTANDING MAIN IDEAS** For each of the following, write the letter of the *best* choice in the space provided.

_____ 1. The sinking of which ship was the first real threat to U.S. neutrality during the early years of World War I?
  a. *Arabic*
  b. *Lusitania*
  c. *Sussex*
  d. *Bremen*

_____ 2. Because they hoped that the war would free Ireland from Great Britain's rule, many Irish Americans initially supported
  a. the Central Powers.
  b. the Allied Powers.
  c. Archduke Franz Ferdinand.
  d. France.

_____ 3. Which former secretary of state believed that American industry's support of the Allies was against the spirit of neutrality?
  a. Woodrow Wilson
  b. Charles Evans Hughes
  c. William Jennings Bryan
  d. Joseph Smith

_____ 4. Diplomatic relations with the United States broke off when the Germans decided to begin full-scale use of their
  a. U-boats.
  b. air force.
  c. artillery.
  d. tanks.

_____ 5. The cable from the German ambassador offering an alliance with Mexico was called the
  a. Richtenhofer Release.
  b. Zimmermann Note.
  c. Lusitania Letter.
  d. Veracruz Communication.

_____ 6. The lack of interest among American men to join the military led to the passage of the
  a. Folsom Act.
  b. Eighteenth Amendment.
  c. Selective Service Act.
  d. Logan Act.

_____ 7. Who were blocked from joining the marines and generally assigned kitchen duties even though more than 370,000 of their men had been recruited by the U.S. armed forces?
  a. German Americans
  b. African Americans
  c. Chinese Americans
  d. Italian Americans

_____ 8. The first U.S. troops landed in France in 1917 under the command of
  a. Lieutenant Edward F. Graham.
  b. Commodore George Dewey.
  c. General John J. Pershing.
  d. General Harry R. Richmond.

_____ 9. The Red Cross, the YMCA, and hospitals all benefited from the thousands of volunteers who were
  a. women.
  b. children.
  c. military advisers.
  d. immigrants.

_____ 10. Merchant vessels transporting war material and personnel were protected by U.S. warships in something called a
  a. transportation plan.
  b. simple maneuver.
  c. sailing fortress.
  d. convoy system.

Main Idea Activities

CHAPTER 12

World War I

MAIN IDEA ACTIVITIES 12.3

■ VOCABULARY

An expression to understand:

• **wheatless days (369):** days in which foods made from wheat, like bread, were not eaten

Other terms:

• **propaganda (368):** spreading information as fact that reflects the particular views and interests of the people supporting the information

• **commodities (369):** goods that are used for trade or commerce

• **allocating (369):** setting something apart for a special purpose

• **massive (373):** huge

• **upbeat (370):** optimistic; cheerful

■ CLASSIFYING INFORMATION Complete the chart about U.S. wartime boards, using the following items.

• Herbert Hoover
• Railroad Administration
• William McAdoo

• Harry Garfield
• farm production increased
• limited transportation rates

• Food Administration
• temporarily closed coal plants
• Fuel Administration

U.S. Wartime Boards

Board	• _____	• _____	• _____
Leader	• _____	• _____	• _____
Achievement	• _____ _____ _____ _____	• _____ _____ _____ _____	• _____ _____ _____ _____

■ **REVIEWING FACTS** **Choose the correct items from the following list to complete the statements below.**

War Industries	Nineteenth Amendment	Committee on Public Information
labor	Liberty bonds	Juliette Gordon Low
volunteerism	women	Great Migration
Bernard Baruch	liberty pups	Espionage and Sedition Acts

1. One of the ways the government successfully raised money for the war was through the sale

   of _____.

2. The _____ Board was established to coordinate the work
   of all the other government wartime boards.

3. Taking advantage of a desperate shortage of _____, the
   unionized workers went on strike across the nation to force improvement of working conditions.

4. Because many skilled craftsmen were away at war, it became common for

   _____ to take over jobs like automobile mechanic, brick-
   layer, and railroad engineer.

5. The involvement of so many women in the war effort resulted in the passage of the

   _____, which gave them the right to vote.

6. Conserving energy, planting victory gardens, and recycling needed materials were all examples

   of the strong _____ that existed throughout the war years.

7. _____ 's work with the Girl Scouts encouraged them to
   throw all of their energies into helping in the war effort.

8. The _____ was a response to the job and wage opportunities southern African Americans saw in the industries of the North.

9. President Wilson began the _____ to try to sell the war
   effort to those Americans who still believed that the United States should have stayed neutral.

10. Wall Street investor _____ was the director of the War
    Industries Board.

11. An example of anti-German sentiment becoming ridiculous was the change of a German-

    sounding word like *dachshunds* to _____.

12. Even though the Supreme Court disagreed, many Americans felt the

    _____ violated the First Amendment guaranteeing the
    right of free speech.

CHAPTER 12 World War I

MAIN IDEA ACTIVITIES 12.4

■ VOCABULARY

An expression to understand:

• **last-ditch (376):** the final attempt

Other terms:

• **gramophones (375):** mechanical record players

• **jauntily (375):** appearing to be confident of oneself

• **deadlock (375):** a standstill that is the result of two sides pushing on each other with the same force

• **forging (377):** pushing ahead

• **incomprehensible (381):** impossible to understand

• **habitable (381):** fit to be lived in

■ CLASSIFYING INFORMATION Determine whether the following statements from Wilson's Fourteen Points were territorial dispute issues or self-determination issues by placing an *X* in the correct column.

Wilson's Fourteen Points	Territorial Disputes	Self-Determination
Belgium must be evacuated and restored.		
People of Austria-Hungary should be accorded the opportunity of autonomous development.		
Readjust the frontiers of Italy along clearly recognizable lines of nationality.		
Romania, Serbia, and Montenegro should be evacuated.		

■ EVALUATING INFORMATION Mark each statement *T* if it is true or *F* if it is false.

_____ **1.** The League of Nations was at the heart of Wilson's Fourteen Points program.

_____ **2.** At the peace conference in Europe, the Big Four demanded that Germany pay huge amounts of money to the Allies to pay back the costs of the war.

_____ **3.** The Treaty of Versailles was very positive toward the Germans and the other Central Powers.

_____ **4.** The peace treaty created the new nations of Czechoslovakia and Yugoslavia.

_____ **5.** President Wilson's Fourteen Points were so well liked that very little was changed and they were put into practice almost immediately.

_____ **6.** Wilson agreed to the Treaty of Versailles because he believed that the formation of the League of Nations would address any injustices that might be there.

_____ **7.** Henry Cabot Lodge was a longtime opponent of Woodrow Wilson and leader of the reservationists, who were against approving the Treaty of Versailles.

_____ **8.** One of the biggest blocks to the Senate approval of the Treaty of Versailles was the provision called Article 10.

_____ **9.** World War I destroyed the economies of both the European Allied Power countries and the Central Power countries.

CHAPTER
13

A Turbulent Decade

MAIN IDEA ACTIVITIES 13.1

■ VOCABULARY

Some terms to understand:

• **reeled** (390): spun around

• **hysteria** (393): fear and panic not based on reason

• **tainted** (396): spoiled

■ CLASSIFYING INFORMATION Examine the drawings and then label them using the appropriate following items.

• Steel strike

• Boston Police strike

• Seattle general strike

• United Mine Workers strike

Major Labor Strikes of 1919

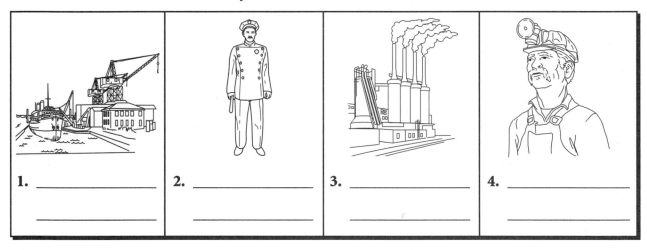

1. _____

2. _____

3. _____

4. _____

■ UNDERSTANDING MAIN IDEAS For each of the following, write the letter of the *best* choice in the space provided.

_____ 1. One of the main factors adding to the problems of postwar demobilization was that the government no longer needed industry to produce material for the
a. school system.
b. Senate.
c. farm industry.
d. military.

_____ 2. Which U.S. city mayor said that the general strike was "of itself the weapon of revolution"?
a. Ole Hanson
b. Eugene Debs
c. Nicolo Sacco
d. John L. Lewis

_____ **3.** Because he believed that their strike was a danger to public safety, Governor Calvin Coolidge called in the state militia during which strike?
   a. United Mine Workers
   b. Boston Police
   c. Steelworkers' Union
   d. Shipyard Workers' Union

_____ **4.** Who was the United Mine Workers' leader whose success helped him become a national labor leader after the 1919 strikes?
   a. John L. Lewis
   b. Edward Curtis
   c. Eugene Debs
   d. Vladimir I. Lenin

_____ **5.** Which 1919 international organization's goals were to overthrow capitalism and free enterprise?
   a. Democratic Union
   b. Communist International
   c. League of Nations
   d. Anarchists' League

_____ **6.** The term used to describe the hysterical fear of a communist revolution in America was the
   a. Yellow Scare.
   b. Green Scare.
   c. White Scare.
   d. Red Scare.

_____ **7.** The fear of radicals became so great that some elected representatives in the New York State Assembly were expelled because they were members of the
   a. Democratic Party.
   b. Socialist Party.
   c. Republican Party.
   d. Progressive Party.

_____ **8.** Between November 1919 and January 1920 federal officials arrested thousands of people suspected of radical beliefs in an action called the
   a. Palmer raids.
   b. Bolshevik directive.
   c. Hoover round-up.
   d. Wilson activities.

_____ **9.** The trial and execution of Sacco and Vanzetti upset many around the world because they believed that the real reason the two were convicted is that they were
   a. Democrats.
   b. New Yorkers.
   c. Republicans.
   d. radicals.

_____ **10.** The deep division in opinion over the Sacco and Vanzetti incident caused American novelist John Dos Passos to say,
   a. "Italians are no good."
   b. "We are two nations."
   c. "Immigration must be controlled."
   d. "Judge Thayer was wrong."

       Main Idea Activities

A Turbulent Decade

CHAPTER 13

MAIN IDEA ACTIVITIES 13.2

■ VOCABULARY

An expression to understand:

• **bowed to pressure (397):** gave in to what they wanted

Other terms:

• **preoccupation (397):** the mind is absorbed in a thought
• **rallied (397):** called together for a common purpose
• **slackening (398):** lessening
• **denounced (401):** criticized; put down; opposed

■ ORGANIZING INFORMATION Complete the chart about the effects of President Harding's policy, using the following items.

• business profits increased
• loss of some Progressive Era labor reforms
• farmers driven deeply into debt
• surplus from tax cuts helped the economy

Effects of President Harding's Policy

Positive	Negative
• _____ _____ • _____ _____	• _____ _____ • _____ _____

■ **REVIEWING FACTS** Choose the correct items from the following list to complete the statements below.

Andrew Mellon	women	League of Women Voters
Alfred E. Smith	farmers	Revenue Act of 1926
oil reserves	yellow-dog contracts	Calvin Coolidge

1. The Fordney-McCumber Tariff Act was intended to help American business but failed to

   help _____ who were also to benefit.

2. Secretary of the Treasury _____ believed that reducing taxes for the wealthy would help the economy because the rich would have more money to invest.

3. One of the reasons membership in the labor unions fell by almost 1.5 million during the Harding administration was because federal courts were upholding

   _____.

4. Formed after passage of the Nineteenth Amendment, the goal of the

   _____ was to make sure that women were aware of public issues and the candidates who were running for office.

5. People who were against the Equal Rights Amendment were afraid that laws protecting

   working conditions for _____ would be overturned.

6. The Teapot Dome scandal involved a Harding administration official selling very profitable

   leases to government-owned _____ in exchange for bribes.

7. The _____ was of great benefit to the wealthy because it resulted in big tax reductions for the rich.

8. The veto of a bill to boost farm prices with government help was an example of the very

   pro-business policies of _____.

9. Even though he lost to Herbert Hoover in 1928, the nomination of presidential candidate

   _____ showed that the Democratic Party was beginning to move in a new direction.

CHAPTER 13

A Turbulent Decade

MAIN IDEA ACTIVITIES 13.3

■ VOCABULARY

Some terms to understand:

- **peak (405):** high point
- **foster (406):** encourage
- **charismatic (407):** a person who can attract others because of a pleasing manner
- **ramshackle (408):** looks like it is about to fall apart
- **anthropologists (409):** scientists who study the development of human beings

■ ORGANIZING INFORMATION Complete the chart by drawing a line from each term or person to the correct picture and using the following items as captions.

- Southwest Pueblo Indians
- Brotherhood of Sleeping Car Porters
- United Negro Improvement Association

Bursum Bill

a. _____
_____

Marcus Garvey

b. _____
_____

A. Philip Randolph

c. _____
_____

■ EVALUATING INFORMATION Mark each statement *T* if it is true or *F* if it is false.

_____ 1. Even in the North, African Americans had to deal with racial discrimination and violence.

_____ 2. The Ku Klux Klan promoted violence and hatred against Catholics, Jews, and immigrants, as well as African Americans.

_____ 3. The Red Scare and increasing immigration were two reasons some Americans initially supported the growth of the Ku Klux Klan.

_____ 4. A 1921 federal antilynching law sponsored by Missouri Representative L. C. Dyer passed with overwhelming support in both the House and the Senate.

_____ 5. When a mob in Waco, Texas, burned a 17-year-old African American to death, W. E. B. Du Bois worked hard to get support for the NAACP's antilynching efforts.

_____ 6. Marcus Garvey was against the movement to establish a new political state in Africa for African Americans because he believed that African Americans should stay and fight for equality in America.

_____ 7. Many Americans mistakenly believed that all immigrants were radicals and that they stole jobs from native-born Americans.

_____ 8. The Immigration Act of 1924 effectively reduced Asian immigration to almost nothing.

_____ 9. Mexicans were also negatively affected by the new immigration laws.

_____ 10. Their successful appeal to the American public helped the Pueblo Indians defeat a bill that would have legalized non-Indian claims to Pueblo land.

_____ 11. Before an act of Congress in 1924, not all American Indians had a right to American citizenship.

The Jazz Age

MAIN IDEA ACTIVITIES 14.1

■ VOCABULARY

Some expressions to understand:

- **done out (417):** so tired as to have no energy left at all
- **traffic jams (419):** too many vehicles trying to move in the same direction at the same time
- **celebrity testimonials (421):** famous people talking in support of a product

Other terms:

- **implementing (415):** putting into practice
- **repetitive (416):** doing the same thing over and over again
- **craze (418):** a short-lived popular fashion
- **bombarded (420):** being told the same message several times
- **billboards (418):** large panels in public places where advertisements are displayed
- **slogans (421):** phrases used in advertising that become associated with one product
- **jingles (421):** slogans in the form of short songs
- **robust (421):** full of health and strength

■ EVALUATING INFORMATION Mark each statement *T* if it is true or *F* if it is false.

_____ 1. Information that was obtained during "time-and-motion" studies helped industry develop better and quicker ways of making products.

_____ 2. The new methods of production in factories gave unskilled workers many opportunities for better jobs.

_____ 3. If workers at Henry Ford's automobile plant wanted to earn the full $5 wage for an eight-hour day, they had to follow company rules at home as well as at work.

_____ 4. Manufacturers eventually designed products that were intended to go out of style after a period of time so that they could replace them with new styles.

_____ 5. Most advertisements were trying to sell to men because they were the ones who had jobs.

_____ 6. "Chain stores" was a name for stores that sold different types of chains that could be used in many ways.

■ **UNDERSTANDING MAIN IDEAS** For each of the following, write the letter of the *best* choice in the space provided.

_____ 1. "Tin Lizzie" was the nickname for a

a.   c.

b.   d.

_____ 2. In 1920 the biggest business in the United States was
  a. railway lines.
  b. oil refineries.
  c. automobiles.
  d. farming.

_____ 3. The assembly line was first used to great success by
  a. Frederick W. Taylor.
  b. Alfred P. Sloan.
  c. Franklin D. Roosevelt.
  d. Henry Ford.

_____ 4. Electric appliances in middle- and upper-class homes allowed people to hire fewer
  a. domestic servants.
  b. landscapers.
  c. factory workers.
  d. teachers.

_____ 5. One of the new activities that the automobile owners enjoyed was
  a. bowling.
  b. baseball.
  c. sight-seeing.
  d. hockey.

_____ 6. Some people were concerned when the automobile became popular because teenagers spent less of their social time
  a. studying.
  b. doing chores.
  c. singing.
  d. with their families.

_____ 7. Because so many automobiles quickly became common on the road, a new problem started with
  a. overheating radiators.
  b. traffic jams.
  c. road racing.
  d. streetlights.

_____ 8. Which General Motors executive introduced the idea of buying an automobile by paying for it over a period of time?
  a. Alfred P. Sloan
  b. Henry Ford
  c. John Chrysler
  d. Frederick W. Taylor

_____ 9. Jingles and slogans were two popular approaches to the new business of
  a. welding.
  b. engineering.
  c. dancing.
  d. advertising.

_____ 10. Eleanor Roosevelt's praise of the product Cream of Wheat was an example of the advertising technique called
  a. celebrity testimonial.
  b. selling high.
  c. planned obsolescence.
  d. chain stores.

The Jazz Age

MAIN IDEA ACTIVITIES 14.2

■ VOCABULARY

Some expressions to understand:

- **bobbed hair (423):** a hairstyle in which the hair length is cut to about jaw level on the sides and a little shorter in the back
- **spindle-legged (427):** very thin legs
- **pigeon-toed (427):** feet that turn toward each other at the toes, causing the person to walk awkwardly

Other terms:

- **speakeasies (422):** places where alcohol was illegally sold and consumed
- **stenographers (423):** people who are skilled in writing shorthand
- **fads (424):** fashions that are taken up for a short period of time
- **portals (425):** doors or openings
- **flocked (425):** went in large numbers
- **pentathlon (427):** a sporting event in which the athlete must compete in five different sports
- **decathlon (427):** a sporting event in which the athlete must compete in 10 different sports
- **spellbound (428):** fascinated or enchanted by something

■ EVALUATING INFORMATION Mark each statement *T* if it is true or *F* if it is false.

_____ **1.** Less alcoholism and fewer alcohol-related deaths were two benefits of the prohibition era.

_____ **2.** Prohibition ended with the passage of the Twenty-first Amendment.

_____ **3.** The young people of the 1920s were anxious to continue in the same traditional way of life as their parents.

_____ **4.** During the 1920s many women began careers in areas traditionally open only to men.

_____ **5.** Lower-class young people began to attend college in the same numbers as those from the middle and upper classes.

_____ **6.** Dance marathons and flagpole sitting are two fads that were popular during the 1920s.

■ **REVIEWING FACTS** Choose the correct items from the following list to complete the statements below.

Charles Lindbergh	commercial	Book-of-the-	Babe Ruth
fundamentalism	Scopes Trial	Month-Club	professional sports
revivalist	*The Jazz Singer*	radio	

1. WWJ from Detroit and KDKA from Pittsburgh were the first

   _____ radio stations.

2. Because the _____ was so popular, people in Los Angeles could be listening to the same news, entertainment programs, and advertising as people in New York.

3. _____ from Warner Brothers was the first movie in which the actors' voices were heard.

4. Advances in technology allowed _____ to become one of the most-favored forms of mass entertainment.

5. The _____ was founded in 1923 for the many Americans who liked to read for entertainment.

6. A very popular professional baseball player was _____.

7. _____ was the pilot of *Spirit of St. Louis,* in which he made the first nonstop New York to Paris flight in 1927.

8. Aimee Semple McPherson was a very popular _____ who combined a strong Christian message of morality with the glamour of a Hollywood show.

9. _____ was a religious movement that tried to resist what were felt to be damaging moral changes by teaching that Christian doctrine should be accepted without question.

10. The _____ was a very important event of the time because it exposed deep differences between Americans with traditional religious values and Americans with "modern" values.

■ **INTERPRETING VISUAL IMAGES** Examine the drawing of the flapper and answer the question below.

What are three differences in style between the modern woman of the 1920s and the traditionally dressed woman?

- _____
- _____
- _____

CHAPTER 14 · The Jazz Age

MAIN IDEA ACTIVITIES 14.3

■ VOCABULARY

Some terms to understand:

- **renaissance (430):** a rebirth or revival
- **hybrid (430):** something that is composed of different things
- **heartfelt (430):** sincere
- **slurred (430):** to glide over musical notes rather than singing or playing each one
- **solos (431):** playing an instrument by itself
- **quibble (433):** to criticize or argue over small issues
- **skeptical (435):** doubtful
- **realtor (435):** person who sells real estate
- **mural (436):** a very large image painted or applied directly to a wall or ceiling

■ CLASSIFYING INFORMATION Complete the chart about the Harlem Renaissance by placing the following names under the correct category.

- Paul Robeson
- Louis Armstrong
- Claude McKay
- Bessie Smith
- Langston Hughes
- Rose McClendon

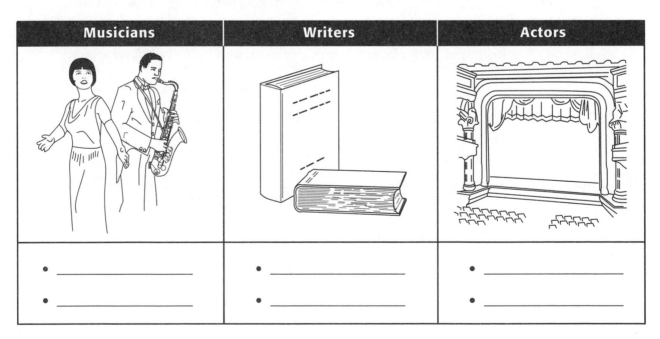

Musicians	Writers	Actors
• _____	• _____	• _____
• _____	• _____	• _____

▪▪ REVIEWING FACTS Choose the correct items from the following list to complete the statements below.

Cotton Club	Lost Generation	Diego Rivera
jazz	George Gershwin	skyscrapers
equal rights	Mexican Renaissance	Frank Lloyd Wright
middle-class	Alfred Stieglitz	Empire State

1. The musical style known as _____ is a blend of many different types of music that were popular in New Orleans in the early 1900s.

2. _____ was a classically trained musician who used the jazz style in his famous composition for orchestra, *Rhapsody in Blue.*

3. One of the most well-known of the Harlem jazz clubs, the _____, attracted some of the best jazz musicians of the age.

4. James Weldon Johnson was one of the most active supporters of the Harlem Renaissance because he believed that developing African American artistic talent would help them achieve _____.

5. Boredom and frustration with the values of postwar American society were highlighted by the writers of the _____.

6. To 1920s journalist and critic Henry L. Mencken, _____ American values were more than worthy of his ridicule.

7. _____ was one of the photographers of the 1920s who was responsible for helping people to see photographs as art.

8. Well-known for his murals describing workers' problems and industrial development, _____ offended some Americans because of his radical politics.

9. *Los tres grandes,* or the big three, refers to three artists who were part of the _____ that also took place during the 1920s.

10. Designer of some of the nation's first _____, Louis Sullivan believed that each part of a building's structure should have a real purpose.

11. The flat landscape of the prairies was the inspiration for _____'s "prairie style" design.

12. Completed in 1931, the _____ Building was the tallest building in the world until 1954.

The Great Depression

CHAPTER 15

MAIN IDEA ACTIVITIES 15.1

■ VOCABULARY

Some expressions to understand:

• **gloomy voices (443):** warning of something bad about to happen

• **debt-ridden (444):** having a lot of debts

• **trim inventories (445):** reduce the amount of products that you have stored

• **fiscal planning (447):** planning of finances or things relating to finances — such as government revenue

■ ORGANIZING INFORMATION Complete the graphic organizer of the steps to the Great Depression by listing the following items in chronological order.

• More banks fail.

• Panicky customers withdraw money.

• Borrowers cannot repay bank loans.

• Some banks fail.

• Stock market crashes.

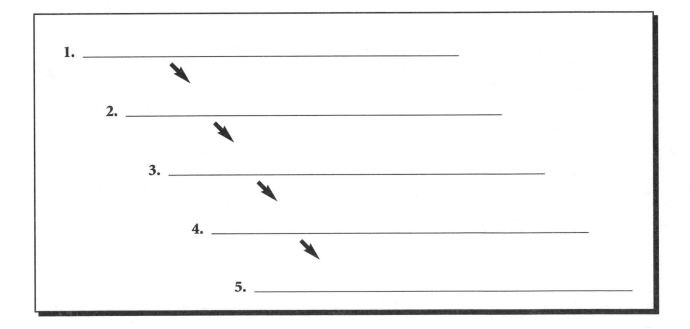

1. _____

2. _____

3. _____

4. _____

5. _____

■ UNDERSTANDING MAIN IDEAS For each of the following, write the letter of the *best* choice in the space provided.

_____ **1.** In the 1920s people could buy more goods than they had the money for because businesses encouraged them to buy
  a. savings bonds.
  b. insurance policies.
  c. on credit.
  d. treasury notes.

_____ **2.** What animal represents a market in which the prices of stocks keep moving up?

  a.  **c.**

  b.  **d.**

_____ **3.** By the end of 1929, the losses in the stock market were more than the United States had spent for
  a. World War I.
  b. the presidential campaign.
  c. political reform.
  d. the Civil War.

_____ **4.** When the banks failed, consumers could no longer afford to buy goods, which severely hurt
  a. professional sports.
  b. industry.
  c. education.
  d. immigration.

_____ **5.** Without a need for high production levels, businesses laid off more and more people, which caused a national problem with
  a. illness.
  b. agriculture.
  c. city planning.
  d. unemployment.

_____ **6.** Huge war debts suffered by European countries after World War I were an important factor in creating
  a. European commerce.
  b. global depression.
  c. changes in social class.
  d. more armies.

_____ **7.** Even though the early 1920s seemed to be good times for everyone, the majority of people saw their incomes go down by
  a. 4 percent.
  b. 2 percent.
  c. 3 percent.
  d. 1 percent.

_____ **8.** Many economists believe that the depression could have been avoided if U.S. workers had gotten
  a. better wages.
  b. health insurance.
  c. the Equal Rights Amendment.
  d. stocks.

_____ **9.** Some type of a depression over a period of time is normal in a free-enterprise economy according to
  a. taxation theory.
  b. business-cycle theory.
  c. legal theory.
  d. finance theory.

CHAPTER
15

The Great Depression

MAIN IDEA ACTIVITIES 15.2

■ VOCABULARY

An expression to understand:

• **golden age (455):** a period of time in which there is great happiness, peace, and prosperity

Other terms:

• **greengrocer (448):** a person who sells fresh fruit and vegetables

• **subsequent (448):** later

• **bedraggled (449):** ragged

• **evicted (450):** forced out; made to leave

• **mainstay (452):** the chief support of something

• **dawdling (454):** taking more time than necessary to do something

• **scrimping (454):** trying to get by on very little

• **utopia (455):** a place where everything is perfect

■ ORGANIZING INFORMATION Complete the chart below about popular culture during the Great Depression.

Popular Culture During the Great Depression

Main Idea Activities

■ **REVIEWING FACTS** Choose the correct items from the following list to complete the statements below.

Hoovervilles	cities	birthrate
hope	Bronx Slave Market	farmers
roles	skilled craftsmen	Mexicans
immigration	African Americans	financial stability

1. The extreme levels of unemployment during the depression resulted in a large decrease in

   the levels of _____ to the United States.

2. In Chicago, a study showed that some people believed that _____
   should not be hired if there were any white workers who were looking for a job.

3. Two African American women described domestic servants standing on street corners look-

   ing for day work as the _____.

4. The poverty of the depression affected people from all walks of life, so it was not uncom-

   mon to find _____ in the breadlines along with everyone else.

5. Long-term health problems due to starvation became a particular problem for people in the

   _____.

6. During the depression, many homeless people blamed the president for not doing enough

   to help, so they called the shantytowns they lived in _____.

7. In certain areas of the country, _____ would be forced to let crops
   rot in the field because they could not find buyers for their produce.

8. In the Southwest and in California, the harsh times of the depression caused an increase in

   discrimination and terrible working conditions for _____.

9. Often, the change in family members' _____ would put a painful
   strain on depression-era marriages.

10. Because the depression caused many couples to delay marriage or remain single, the

    _____ went down.

11. In addition to homelessness, hunger, and joblessness, many Americans suffered psychologi-

    cally because of the serious loss of _____ that things would ever
    improve.

12. A very strong desire for future _____ was one of the effects of the
    depression on the generation of people who grew up during the era.

The Great Depression

MAIN IDEA ACTIVITIES 15.3

■ VOCABULARY

An expression to understand:

• **buying power (460):** having the financial means to make purchases

Other terms:

• **unchecked (458):** uncontrolled; running free

• **marshalled (458):** brought together in an effective way

• **surplus (459):** more than what is needed

• **awkward (459):** not graceful

• **purge (461):** to remove all the impurities from something

• **aloof (461):** being at a distance emotionally

• **earnest (462):** characterized by a serious state of mind

■ ORGANIZING INFORMATION Complete the chart below about Hoover's programs during the Great Depression, using the following items.

• encourage donations to private relief organizations

• purchase surplus farm products

• reduce foreclosures on homes and farms

• stabilize troubled financial institutions

Reconstruction Finance Corporation	• _____ _____
Federal Farm Board	• _____ _____
Home Loan Bank Act	• _____ _____
President's Commission for Unemployment Relief	• _____ _____

■ EVALUATING INFORMATION Mark each statement *T* if it is true or *F* if it is false.

_____ 1. President Hoover believed that the federal government should take an active role in providing direct help in the form of food, housing, and money to people suffering from the effects of the depression.

_____ 2. "Rugged individualism" was President Hoover's term for the idea that individual effort is what is needed to succeed.

_____ 3. President Hoover was known for often changing his mind and direction concerning the depression and how best to handle it.

_____ 4. The Hoover Dam was the result of one of the largest public works efforts supported by President Hoover.

■ REVIEWING FACTS Choose the correct items from the following list to complete the statements below.

capitalism   Salvation Army   Federal Emergency Relief Board
Congress   depression   Franklin D. Roosevelt
army

1. During the early years of the depression, the _____ was one of the charitable organizations that did the most to provide aid to the general public in the form of food and shelter.

2. Even though President Hoover did not support it, two senators tried to pass a bill in 1931 to

    create the _____, which would give states money to provide direct aid to the unemployed.

3. Because they believed that _____ caused the depression, both the Communist Party and the Socialist Party organized mass protests against the government.

4. President Hoover's response to the demands of the Bonus Army was to send in the

    _____ to remove some World War I veterans and their families from empty government buildings.

5. Although born into a very wealthy family, Democratic presidential candidate

    _____ was very much influenced by progressivism and a commitment to public service.

6. The main issue of the 1932 presidential campaign was the

    _____.

7. Because the Democrats won important majorities in _____, FDR knew that his programs likely would receive the legislative support they needed.

★
★
CHAPTER
16

The New Deal

MAIN IDEA ACTIVITIES 16.1

■ VOCABULARY

An expression to understand:

• **drew up (468):** wrote out

Other terms:

• **massive (468):** very large number

• **confidence (469):** trust

• **plight (469):** problems

• **revitalizing (472):** restoring; bringing back to life

• **sought (472):** searched for; tried

■ EVALUATING INFORMATION Mark each statement *T* if it is true or *F* if it is false.

_____ **1.** Herbert Hoover followed Franklin D. Roosevelt as president.

_____ **2.** President Roosevelt's New Deal was a series of 15 measures to help the United States recover from three years of depression.

_____ **3.** The bank holiday was designed to stop people from withdrawing large amounts of money from the banks.

_____ **4.** The Emergency Banking Act authorized the federal government to open new banks.

_____ **5.** President Roosevelt's radio broadcasts came to be known as his "fireside chats."

■ REVIEWING FACTS Choose the correct items from the following list to complete the statements below.

Civil Works Administration

Home Owners Loan Corporation

Federal Deposit Insurance Corporation

Agricultural Adjustment Administration

Federal Emergency Relief Administration

Farm Credit Administration

1. The _____ insured bank deposits up to a certain amount.

2. The _____ provided low-interest, long-term loans to farmers.

3. Home owners who could not meet their mortgage payments were aided by the

_____.

4. The _____ gave $500 million in relief aid to state and local agencies.

5. Government funded jobs were created by the _____.

6. Farmers were paid to reduce their output of products by the _____.

▓▓ UNDERSTANDING MAIN IDEAS For each of the following, write the letter of the *best* choice in the space provided.

_____ **1.** President Roosevelt organized an advisory group called the
   a. President's Trust.
   b. Brain Trust.
   c. Trust Group.
   d. Brain Group.

_____ **2.** Roosevelt hoped that the bank holiday would
   a. give bank employees a rest.
   b. get the bank vaults cleaned out.
   c. restore order to the disagreeing bank presidents.
   d. restore public confidence in the banking system.

_____ **3.** Which of these jobs was not a duty of the Civilian Conservation Corps?
   a. planting trees
   b. creating park trails
   c. building dams
   d. developing campgrounds

_____ **4.** What was President Roosevelt's long-term goal?
   a. recovery
   b. relief
   c. reward
   d. research

_____ **5.** Which of these flags was the NRA banner?

   a. [image of American flag]   **c.** [image of Canadian flag]

   b. [image of Texas flag]   **d.** NRA — U.S. — WE DO OUR PART

_____ **6.** The largest of all the New Deal programs was the
   a. Tennessee Valley Authority.
   b. National Industrial Recovery Act.
   c. Public Works Administration.
   d. National Recovery Administration.

_____ **7.** President Roosevelt appointed more than _____ African Americans to posts in the federal government.
   a. 100
   b. 250
   c. 500
   d. 1,000

CHAPTER 16

The New Deal

MAIN IDEA ACTIVITIES 16.2

■ VOCABULARY

Some terms to understand:

- **pension (475):** regular payment of money
- **polio (476):** disease that often paralyzes people
- **legitimate (480):** lawful; justified

■ ORGANIZING INFORMATION Complete the chart below about agencies set up during the New Deal.

New Deal Agencies

Abbreviation	Name	Purpose
1. FCA	_____	_____
2. _____	Civilian Conservation Corps	_____
3. _____	_____	To construct power plants
4. HOLC	_____	_____
5. NRA	_____	_____
6. _____	_____	To construct roads
7. _____	Securities and Exchange Commission	_____
8. _____	_____	To provide electricity
9. AAA	_____	_____

███ **EVALUATING INFORMATION** Mark each statement *T* if it is true or *F* if it is false.

_____ **1.** Francis E. Townsend wanted the U.S. government to give a pension of $200 a month to every American over 60 years old.

_____ **2.** The Share-Our-Wealth program would give the government the right to tax the poor and give the money to the rich.

_____ **3.** Congress passed the Share-Our-Wealth program in 1935.

_____ **4.** The Second New Deal included more public-works programs, a social security plan, and improvements for laborers.

_____ **5.** The Works Progress Administration was designed to help Americans find work.

_____ **6.** The National Youth Administration found places for homeless children to live.

_____ **7.** The Rural Electrification Administration provided electricity to isolated rural areas.

_____ **8.** The Revenue Act of 1935 was often called the Poor Tax Act.

_____ **9.** The Revenue Act of 1935 increased taxes on the nation's richest people.

_____ **10.** Roosevelt wanted to replace any Supreme Court justices over the age of 70.

_____ **11.** The Wagner-Connery Act guaranteed laborers the right to organize unions.

_____ **12.** The General Motors strike of 1936–37 lasted for six months.

_____ **13.** The Farm Security Administration provided low-interest, long-term loans to help tenant farmers and sharecroppers buy land.

CHAPTER
16

The New Deal

MAIN IDEA ACTIVITIES 16.3

▮ VOCABULARY

Some terms to understand:

- **spurred (482):** urged or pushed
- **natural disaster (482):** terrible event that is not caused by humans, such as a tornado or drought
- **grim (484):** sad; troubling
- **documentary (484):** presentation of factual information
- **dignity (484):** self-respect
- **scavenged (484):** searched for

▮ ORGANIZING INFORMATION Complete the graphic organizer below by listing three ways that government-funded jobs benefited the people.

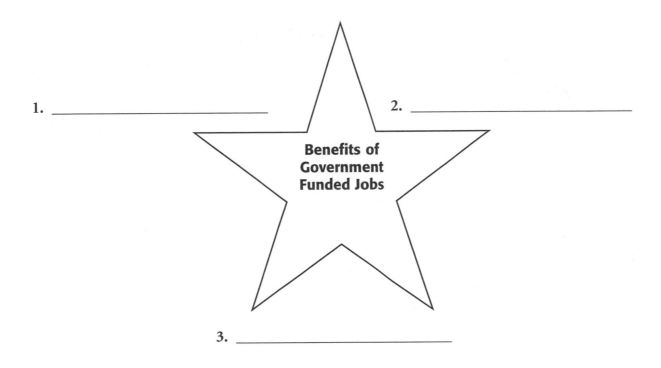

1. _____

2. _____

Benefits of Government Funded Jobs

3. _____

▮▮ REVIEWING FACTS Choose the correct item from the following list to complete each statement below.

National Youth Administration	Agriculture	Field Workers Union
federal government	drought	Dorothea Lange
Mexican Americans	electricity	trees

1. In the mid-1930s a severe _____ struck the Great Plains.

2. The Department of _____ started programs to conserve soil.

3. Over 200 million _____ were planted to create a windbreak from Texas to Canada.

4. _____ and Filipinos were often victims of discrimination in many New Deal programs.

5. The _____ was an organization for Mexican American and Filipino laborers.

6. Most of the photographers working on documentaries at this time were hired by the

   _____.

7. _____ was one of the most talented photographers of the depression era. She was noted for her photo *Migrant Mother*.

8. Programs sponsored by the _____ enabled children to stay in school.

9. Providing _____ to rural areas had a great impact on many people's lives.

The New Deal

CHAPTER
16

MAIN IDEA ACTIVITIES 16.4

■ VOCABULARY

Some terms to understand:

- **arts (487):** music, dance, theater, or literature
- **folk (487):** ethnic group or race of people

■ ORGANIZING INFORMATION Complete the graphic organizer using the following book titles.

- *Their Eyes Were Watching God*
- *Gone With the Wind*
- *The Grapes of Wrath*
- *Native Son*

1. _____
   the story of a poor family traveling from the Dust Bowl region to California

2. _____
   a black woman's search for fulfillment in rural Florida

3. _____
   the journey of a young African American man lost in a racist world in which he can never succeed

4. _____
   a story of the Old South set during the Civil War and Reconstruction

■ CLASSIFYING INFORMATION Mark each of the following parts of Federal Project Number One with either *A* (arts), *M* (music), *T* (theater), or *W* (writers).

_____ **1.** Paint murals on public buildings.

_____ **2.** Produce state travel guides.

_____ **3.** Produce histories of ethnic groups.

_____ **4.** Teach art in public schools.

_____ **5.** Form orchestras.

_____ **6.** Bring live theater to small towns.

_____ **7.** Hire actors, directors, and playwrights.

_____ **8.** Present 4,000 productions each month.

_____ **9.** Produce posters for the New Deal programs.

■ REVIEWING FACTS Choose the correct item from the following list to complete the statements below.

Swing	Gospel music	regionalists
Aaron Copland	Lillian Hellman	
The Petrified Forest	*Grand Ole Opry*	

1. Robert Sherwood's play _____ was about ideas that were destroying the country.

2. *The Little Foxes* was a play by _____ that attacked upper-class greed.

3. _____ used American folk songs and folktales as the basis for many popular songs.

4. The _____ was a radio show that helped to popularize country music.

5. _____ is a cross between traditional spirituals and jazz.

6. _____ was a smooth, big-band style of music, popular in dance halls.

7. Midwestern artists who stressed local folk themes and customs were called

_____.

CHAPTER 17

The Road to War

MAIN IDEA ACTIVITIES 17.1

■ VOCABULARY

Some terms to understand:

- **shun (502):** stay away from
- **diplomacy (503):** keeping peace by negotiating agreements
- **moratorium (506):** temporary suspension of payments

■ ORGANIZING INFORMATION Complete the chart about treaties from the Washington Conference by writing the correct name of each treaty.

Treaty	Provisions
1. _____ _____	The United States, Great Britain, and Japan would destroy some of their warships in order to limit their naval strength.
2. _____ _____	Britain, France, Japan, and the United States pledged to respect one another's territory in the Pacific.
3. _____ _____	It guaranteed China's territorial integrity and promised to uphold the Open Door Policy.

■ EVALUATING INFORMATION Mark each statement *T* if it is true or *F* if it is false.

_____ **1.** After World War I, all U.S. senators agreed to join the League of Nations.

_____ **2.** Most people believed that World War I had made the world safe for democracy.

_____ **3.** The World Court was created to resolve international disputes.

_____ **4.** Reducing the size of a country's military is called disarmament.

_____ **5.** The main goals of the Washington Conference were naval disarmament and Pacific security.

_____ **6.** The Kellogg-Briand Pact outlawed war of any kind.

_____ **7.** Adolf Hitler was convinced that politicians were responsible for Germany losing the war.

CHAPTER 17 The Road to War

MAIN IDEA ACTIVITIES 17.2

VOCABULARY

An expression to understand:

• **mutual respect (508):** consideration that is shown by two parties to each other

Other terms:

• **intervene (508):** step in; interfere

• **banana republics (509):** countries that were run to benefit foreign companies

• **seizure (509):** taking control of something; capturing

ORGANIZING INFORMATION Complete the chart of Nicaraguan events by placing the following items in chronological order.

• Augusto César Sandino refused to accept Stimson's proposal.

• The United States refused to accept Chamorro's government.

• Sandino organized a revolt against Chamorro and Adolfo Díaz.

• General Anastasio Somoza ordered Sandino's assassination.

• Emiliano Chamorro overthrew the Nicaraguan government, which started a bitter civil war.

• Somoza forced out the Nicaraguan president and took over the presidency.

• President Coolidge ordered the U.S. Marines to protect American commercial interests in Nicaragua.

• Stimson helped negotiate a peace treaty in May 1927.

• President Coolidge sent Henry Stimson to negotiate an end to the civil war.

Events in Nicaragua

1. _____	4. _____	7. _____
2. _____	5. _____	8. _____
3. _____	6. _____	9. _____

■ **REVIEWING FACTS** **Choose the correct item from the following list to complete the statements below.**

Caudillos   Cuba   nationalize
United Fruit Company   economic depression
President Hoover   Good Neighbor policy

1. Before his inauguration, _____ toured Latin America to promote friendly relations with the countries.

2. President Roosevelt's policy of respecting the rights of other countries was called the

   _____.

3. In 1934 President Roosevelt signed a treaty with _____ that said the United States would not interfere in its affairs.

4. The _____ owned millions of acres of farmland in Central America and the Caribbean.

5. In 1938 Mexico's president began to _____, or assert government control over, the country's oil industry.

6. From 1929 to 1930 there was unrest in Latin America due to a(n)

   _____.

7. _____ were Latin American military leaders who used force to maintain order.

CHAPTER 17

The Road to War

MAIN IDEA ACTIVITIES 17.3

■ VOCABULARY

Some terms to understand:

- **clashes (512):** fights
- **Third Reich (513):** Hitler's government
- **suffrage (514):** voting rights
- **incompatible (514):** unable to get along

■ ORGANIZING INFORMATION Complete the chart about the ideas or policies of Hitler, Mussolini, and Stalin, using the following items.

- reorganized private land into farms run by the government
- prohibited Jews and non-Nazis from holding government positions
- blamed Jews and Communists for Germany's decline
- limited freedom of speech

- sent protesters to labor camps
- arrested political opponents
- outlawed strikes
- made military service mandatory
- restricted voting rights

Hitler	Mussolini	Stalin
1. _____	1. _____	1. _____
2. _____	2. _____	2. _____
3. _____	3. _____	
4. _____		

■ UNDERSTANDING MAIN IDEAS For each of the following, write the letter of the *best* choice in the space provided.

_____ **1.** Benito Mussolini rose to power in
    a. France.
    b. Italy.
    c. Germany.
    d. the Soviet Union.

_____ **2.** Benito Mussolini founded the
    a. Fascist Party.
    b. Nazi Party.
    c. Republican Party.
    d. Socialist Party.

_____ **3.** That military-dominated government should control all aspects of
society was the belief of the
   a. Fascist Party.
   b. Nazi Party.
   c. Republican Party.
   d. Socialist Party.

_____ **4.** Mussolini's army was called the
   a. Redcoats.
   b. Blackshirts.
   c. Blackboots.
   d. Fascist Army.

_____ **5.** Mussolini gained control of
_____ in 1935.
   a. France
   b. Brazil
   c. Ethiopia
   d. England

_____ **6.** The Soviet Union was formed
from _____ and several surrounding states.
   a. Germany
   b. Great Britain
   c. Brazil
   d. Russia

_____ **7.** Joseph Stalin rose to power in
   a. Italy.
   b. Germany.
   c. France.
   d. the Soviet Union.

_____ **8.** Stalin belonged to the
   a. Communist Party.
   b. Fascist Party.
   c. Nazi Party.
   d. Socialist Party.

_____ **9.** Stalin's army was called the
   a. Black Army.
   b. Red Coats.
   c. Blackshirts.
   d. Red Army.

_____ **10.** Hitler rose to power in
   a. France.
   b. Italy.
   c. the Soviet Union.
   d. Germany.

_____ **11.** Hitler's storm troopers were
called
   a. Blackshirts.
   b. Brownshirts.
   c. Red Coats.
   d. Brown Army.

_____ **12.** Anti-Semitism is the hatred of
   a. Jews.
   b. Germans.
   c. Seminole Indians.
   d. Catholics.

_____ **13.** The _____ deprived Jews of
their German citizenship and
authorized the destruction of
Jewish property.
   a. Property Laws
   b. Jewish Law
   c. Nuremberg Laws
   d. Semitism Laws

_____ **14.** The Spanish Civil War was fought
between Loyalists and
   a. Nazis.
   b. Socialists.
   c. Fascists.
   d. Communists.

_____ **15.** Franco rose to power in
   a. Spain.
   b. France.
   c. Germany.
   d. Italy.

_____ **16.** In 1931 Manchuria was invaded
and taken over by
   a. Germany.
   b. Italy.
   c. the Soviet Union.
   d. Japan.

The Road to War

MAIN IDEA ACTIVITIES 17.4

■ VOCABULARY

Some expressions to understand:

• **puppet government (793):** government that is controlled by another government

• **shoot-on-sight (793):** shoot as soon as you see the person

Other terms:

• **shake-up (790):** unexpected change

• **underestimated (790):** did not realize the great power of

• **remedy (790):** fix; correct

• **munitions (791):** military supplies

• **embargo (795):** order by a government prohibiting the movement of merchant ships into or out of another country's ports

■ ORGANIZING INFORMATION Complete the chart below by listing four components of the Atlantic Charter.

The Atlantic Charter

- _____
  _____

- _____
  _____

- _____
  _____

- _____
  _____

■ EVALUATING INFORMATION Mark each statement *T* if it is true or *F* if it is false.

_____ 1. In 1933 the United States and the Soviet Union became allies as a response to fascism in Europe and Asia.

_____ 2. Germany and Russia formed an alliance known as the Axis Powers.

_____ 3. Giving into demands in an attempt to avoid a larger conflict is called appeasement.

_____ 4. Between 1935 and 1939 Congress passed a series of neutrality laws because America wanted to stay out of other nations' conflicts.

_____ 5. Great Britain and France wanted the Soviet Union's help in defending Poland from Germany.

_____ 6. The Soviet Union joined forces with Great Britain and France.

_____ 7. Stalin and Hitler had a secret agreement to divide Poland between them.

_____ 8. The fighting in Europe was a major issue in the 1940 presidential election.

_____ 9. During the election, Roosevelt promised that the United States would remain neutral.

_____ 10. The Lend-Lease Act appropriated $7 billion for military aid to the Axis countries.

_____ 11. The Resistance was a secret, French organization that opposed the Germans.

_____ 12. In 1940 Winston Churchill became prime minister of France.

_____ 13. On December 7, 1941, Japan attacked the U.S. naval base at Pearl Harbor.

Name _____ Class _____ Date _____

CHAPTER 18 Americans in World War II

MAIN IDEA ACTIVITIES 18.1

■ VOCABULARY

Some terms to understand:

- **barracks (528):** buildings used to house soldiers
- **deferred (530):** excused
- **outnumbered (531):** had more people
- **outgunned (531):** had more guns and ammunition
- **U-boats (531):** German submarines

■ ORGANIZING INFORMATION Complete the chart about Allied and Axis advantages at the time of U.S. entry into World War II, using the following items.

- better prepared for war
- great production capacity
- enemy had to maintain troops on two active fronts
- firm control of invaded areas
- tremendous manpower

Allied Advantages	Axis Advantages
• _____ • _____ • _____	• _____ • _____

■ CLASSIFYING INFORMATION Mark each statement *P* (positive) if it was a positive consequence of the war or *N* (negative) if it was a negative consequence of the war.

_____ **1.** An increase in production created an economic boom that ended the Great Depression.

_____ **2.** Unemployment dropped.

Main Idea Activities

Chapter 18 **121**

_____ **3.** Farmers' crop production increased.

_____ **4.** Nylon and other fabrics used for clothing were scarce.

_____ **5.** Middle- and lower-income groups had to pay income tax.

_____ **6.** Inflation was kept down by the sale of war bonds.

_____ **7.** Food and other necessities were rationed.

_____ **8.** Wages were frozen.

■ REVIEWING FACTS Choose the correct items from the following list to complete the statements below.

Battle of the Coral Sea	Battle of Midway	Selective Training and Service Act
Japanese	Chester Nimitz	drafted
Stalingrad	Bataan Death March	Douglas MacArthur

1. The _____ required all men between the ages of 21 to 35 to register for the draft.

2. About two thirds of the men who served during World War II had been

_____.

3. General _____ commanded the U.S. and Filipino troops in the Philippines.

4. _____ soldiers outnumbered and outgunned the inexperienced Allied soldiers.

5. Japanese soldiers led over 70,000 prisoners on the _____ to their prison camp.

6. The commander of the U.S. Pacific Fleet was Admiral _____.

7. The Allies stopped the Japanese advance on Australia at the

_____.

8. The Allies were able to win the _____ because they broke the Japanese fleet code and were aware of their plans.

9. The Axis troops surrendered in late January 1943 at the Battle of

_____.

CHAPTER 18 — Americans in World War II

MAIN IDEA ACTIVITIES 18.2

■ VOCABULARY

An expression to understand:

• **victory gardens (536):** backyard vegetable gardens grown during World War II

Other terms:

• **sacrifices (535):** things that are given up

• **radically (536):** in an extreme manner

• **sentimental (537):** emotional

• **surpass (537):** move beyond

• **biased (540):** prejudiced; slanted to an unfair point of view

■ EVALUATING INFORMATION   Mark each statement *T* if it is true or *F* if it is false.

_____ **1.** President Wilson gave the famous Four Freedoms Speech.

_____ **2.** Paperback books were first published during World War II.

_____ **3.** Norman Rockwell became known for his covers of *Life* magazine.

_____ **4.** During World War II the number of women in the workforce decreased.

_____ **5.** Many war plants would not hire African Americans, or would employ them only as janitors.

_____ **6.** During World War II Japanese Americans were forced to move off their property and live in special camps.

■ **UNDERSTANDING MAIN IDEAS** **For each of the following, write the letter of the *best* choice in the space provided.**

_____ **1.** Which of these symbols indicated that the family had a loved one serving in the war?

a.

c.

b.

d.

_____ **2.** West coast cities engaged in blackouts because
  a. they did not want the lights of the city to create a target.
  b. they wanted to save energy.
  c. it was a way of mourning the deaths caused by war.
  d. everyone went to bed early.

_____ **3.** Which of these was *NOT* a freedom of President Roosevelt's Four Freedoms Speech?
  a. freedom of speech and expression
  b. freedom to worship God in one's own way
  c. freedom from rules or laws
  d. freedom from fear

_____ **4.** The 88th Division was a combat unit made up mostly of
  a. African Americans.
  b. Native Americans.
  c. Japanese prisoners of war.
  d. Mexican Americans.

Americans in World War II

CHAPTER 18

MAIN IDEA ACTIVITIES 18.3

■ VOCABULARY

An expression to understand:

• **annihilation of an entire people (545):** total removal, or killing, of a specific group

Other terms:

• **surf (542):** waves

• **beachhead (543):** shoreline that has been captured by troops in advance of the major attack

• **gateway (543):** entrance

• **armistice (543):** truce

• **bogged (543):** slowed

• **fortified (544):** strengthened

• **ghettos (545):** sections of European cities where Jews were forced to live

• **anti-Semitism (546):** hatred of Jews

• **unprecedented (548):** had not happened before

■ ORGANIZING INFORMATION Complete the chart about Operation Overlord by writing the following steps in chronological order.

• The Allies had moved 20 miles into France by early July.

• The Allies left clues to make it look like the invasion would take place near Calais, on the English Channel.

• The Allies liberated Paris on August 25, 1944.

• The Allies landed in Normandy on June 6, 1944, with many troops.

• Hitler refused to send reinforcements for the Axis troops.

• The Allies bombed roads, bridges, and German troops.

Operation Overlord

1. _____

2. _____

3. _____

4. _____

5. _____

6. _____

▪ REVIEWING FACTS Choose the correct item from the following list to complete the statements below.

Wehrmacht   Holocaust   Adolf Hitler
Japan   Rome   Operation Overlord
Yalta Conference   sonar equipment   Battle of the Bulge

1. The first Axis capital to fall was _____.

2. The refinement of _____ helped the Allies in the Battle of the Atlantic.

3. _____ means German armed forces.

4. The Allied invasion of German-occupied France was called _____.

5. The _____ was Nazi Germany's systematic slaughter of European Jews.

6. The _____ was Germany's final counterattack.

7. The _____ was a meeting between President Franklin D. Roosevelt, Winston Churchill, and Joseph Stalin to plan postwar peace.

8. Stalin pledged to declare war on _____ three months after Germany's surrender.

9. On April 30, 1945, _____ committed suicide.

CHAPTER 18

Americans in World War II

MAIN IDEA ACTIVITIES 18.4

■ VOCABULARY

Some terms to understand:

- **strategic (549):** important in the winning of a war
- **atomic bomb (553):** bomb that gets its power from nuclear energy
- **vaporized (554):** turned into a gas
- **spontaneously ignited (554):** caught on fire from something already on fire
- **combustible (554):** being able to burn

■ ORGANIZING INFORMATION Complete the chart about the significance of the capture of islands in the Pacific during World War II by listing a reason for their importance to the Allied forces.

Significance of Island Capture

Tarawa	Marshall Islands
• _____ _____ _____	• _____ _____ _____

■ CLASSIFYING INFORMATION Mark these statements as either *J* (justified) or *O* (opposed) to the use of the atomic bomb on Hiroshima.

_____ **1.** Japan refused to surrender unconditionally.

_____ **2.** The use of the bomb had prevented a costly invasion of Japan.

_____ **3.** Tokyo was considering peace negotiations.

_____ **4.** With Soviet help, victory would have been possible without the bomb.

_____ **5.** The Japanese started the war; they have been paid back manyfold.

_____ **6.** The bomb was dropped to strengthen the U.S. postwar position.

_____ **7.** Top military leaders in Tokyo strongly opposed plans for peace.

■ EVALUATING INFORMATION Mark each statement *T* if it is true or *F* if it is false.

_____ **1.** The island of Tarawa was difficult to capture because of a coral reef.

_____ **2.** The Battle of Iwo Jima lasted six months.

_____ **3.** On April 1, 1945, the largest landing force in Pacific history invaded Okinawa.

_____ **4.** The Battle of Okinawa was the bloodiest battle of the Pacific.

_____ **5.** Japanese soldiers hid in trees and shot at U.S. soldiers as they passed by.

_____ **6.** The Manhattan Project was a group of scientists working on developing a bomb.

_____ **7.** The atomic bomb was dropped on Hiroshima because Japan had refused to surrender.

_____ **8.** A second atomic bomb was dropped on Tokyo.

_____ **9.** Japan surrendered on September 2, 1945.

_____ **10.** World War II resulted in more deaths and destroyed more property than any other war in history.

Main Idea Activities

The Cold War

MAIN IDEA ACTIVITIES 19.1

■ VOCABULARY

Some terms to understand:

- **corrugated (560):** describes a material that has alternating ridges and grooves
- **atrocities (562):** terrible behaviors; unspeakable acts
- **tribunal (562):** court
- **delegates (563):** people chosen to act as representatives
- **instrumental (564):** had an important role in doing something
- **exiled (565):** forced to live outside of one's own country

■ ORGANIZING INFORMATION Complete the graphic organizer by listing the charges German officials faced at the Nuremberg Trials.

1. _____

   _____

2. _____

   _____

Nuremberg Trial Charges

3. _____

   _____

4. _____

   _____

■ EVALUATING INFORMATION Mark each statement *T* if it is true or *F* if it is false.

_____ **1.** After World War II, Germany was divided into four zones. Each zone was to be controlled by a different Allied country.

_____ **2.** The Soviet Union's occupation of Eastern Europe was a source of tension for the Allies.

_____ **3.** The Soviet Union occupied Japan after World War II.

_____ **4.** The International Military Tribunal for the Far East was established to try suspected war criminals from the war in the Pacific.

_____ **5.** The postwar trials set a standard that nations and individuals can be held accountable for their actions during a war.

_____ **6.** The Allies hoped to use the United Nations to continue working for world peace.

_____ **7.** The United Nations proposed to divide Palestine into two states—one for Jews and the other for Arabs.

■ REVIEWING FACTS Choose the correct item from the following list to complete the statements below.

Nuremberg Trials	Potsdam Conference	Israel
Ralph Bunche	Zionism	Palestine
General Assembly	Security Council	United Nations
Latin America	*zaibatsu*	

1. The Allied Powers met at the _____ to decide how to handle postwar Germany.

2. _____ were huge Japanese corporations run by single families that monopolized the economy.

3. The German war crime trials were known as the _____.

4. Some Nazi officials escaped prosecution by fleeing to _____.

5. The organization that was founded after World War II to promote world peace is the

_____.

6. The United Nations _____ focuses on the organization's policies.

7. The United Nations _____ addresses military and political problems.

8. After World War II, many European Jews moved to _____.

9. _____ was the movement for a Jewish homeland in Palestine.

10. Jewish leaders named their portion of Palestine _____.

11. _____, the first African American to receive the Nobel Peace Prize, was honored for his peace-making efforts between the Arabs and Jews in Palestine.

The Cold War

MAIN IDEA ACTIVITIES 19.2

■ VOCABULARY

Some terms to understand:

- **standoff (566):** being unable to work together because of a disagreement
- **rivalry (566):** competition
- **descended (567):** fallen
- **impose (568):** set; place by authority
- **vulnerable (569):** open to attack or damage
- **pledged (571):** promised

■ ORGANIZING INFORMATION Complete the chart below by listing the following items as principles of either the United States or the Soviet Union.

- use of force to overcome opposition
- democratic government
- communism
- capitalist economy

- government of one-party rule
- belief in individual freedom
- suppression of religion
- state-run economy

United States	Soviet Union
• _____	• _____
• _____	• _____
• _____	• _____
	• _____
	• _____

■ UNDERSTANDING MAIN IDEAS For each of the following, write the letter of the *best* choice in the space provided.

_____ 1. The competition between the United States and the Soviet Union was known as the
  a. Powers War.
  b. Competitive War.
  c. Hot War.
  d. Cold War.

_____ 2. The United States had trouble trusting the Soviet Union after World War II because of
  a. Soviet expansion.
  b. Soviet spies.
  c. the Soviet Union's refusal to help pay for war damages.
  d. the Soviet Union's new leaders.

_____ 3. Satellite nations were countries under the control of
  a. the United States.
  b. Great Britain.
  c. France.
  d. the Soviet Union.

_____ 4. Restricting the expansion of Soviet communism was called
  a. restriction.
  b. expansionism.
  c. communism restraint.
  d. containment.

_____ 5. In 1946 Congress passed the Atomic Energy Act which put nuclear weapons and research under _____ control.
  a. civilian
  b. government
  c. religious
  d. military

_____ 6. The _____ aided the West Germans by delivering supplies after the Soviet Union blocked transportation routes from Berlin.
  a. French navy
  b. Berlin Airlift
  c. Berlin railroad
  d. Japanese airforce

_____ 7. Which of these nations did not join NATO and pledge to defend other NATO members in the case of an outside attack?
  a. United States
  b. Canada
  c. Soviet Union
  d. Iceland

The Cold War

MAIN IDEA ACTIVITIES 19.3

■ VOCABULARY

An expression to understand:
• **came to a head** (572): could not be ignored

Other terms:
• **stalemate** (575): situation in which further action by either of the two opponents is impossible
• **covert** (576): secret
• **martial law** (577): temporary rule by military authority
• **jovial** (578): happy

■ EVALUATING INFORMATION Mark each statement *T* if it is true or *F* if it is false.

_____ **1.** In 1911 a group of students in China formed a Communist Party.

_____ **2.** By 1920 civil war had erupted in China between the Nationalists and Communists.

_____ **3.** During World War II, the civil war in China continued.

_____ **4.** After World War II, the conflict between the Nationalists and Communists in China continued.

_____ **5.** President Truman kept a neutral position regarding the Chinese civil war.

_____ **6.** In 1945 the Allies divided Korea into two zones. Soviet troops occupied the north, and U.S. troops occupied the south.

_____ **7.** North Korea invaded South Korea on June 25, 1950.

_____ **8.** The United States did not want South Korea to fall to the Communists, but the United States still remained neutral.

■ CLASSIFYING INFORMATION Mark each item *T* if it was an action of President Truman or *M* if it was an action of General MacArthur.

_____ **1.** called for a major expansion of the Korean War

_____ **2.** strongly opposed expansion of the Korean War

_____ **3.** was worried that expansion might lead to another world war

_____ **4.** refused to accept the Korean War as a limited conflict

_____ **5.** demanded an unconditional surrender from North Korea

_____ **6.** removed MacArthur from his command

_____ **7.** was treated like a hero upon returning to the United States

■ **UNDERSTANDING MAIN IDEAS** For each of the following, write the letter of the *best* choice in the space provided.

_____ **1.** President Truman did not run for re-election in 1952 because
a. he had little support.
b. he became very ill.
c. he died.
d. he had already served two consecutive terms.

_____ **2.** Who did the Republicans choose as their presidential candidate in 1952?
a. Harry S Truman
b. General MacArthur
c. Adlai Stevenson
d. Dwight D. Eisenhower

_____ **3.** The Eisenhower administration viewed technology and _____ as crucial to ending communist expansion.
a. naval bases
b. nuclear arms
c. space exploration
d. manpower

_____ **4.** The offering of military aid, and in some instances U.S. troops, to any Middle East nation seeking help in resisting communist aggression came from the
a. Eisenhower Pledge.
b. Truman Papers.
c. Eisenhower Doctrine.
d. Dulles's Policy.

_____ **5.** In 1959 President Eisenhower and Premier Khrushchev of the Soviet Union agreed to meet to discuss
a. arms reduction.
b. expansion.
c. the Korean War.
d. space exploration.

_____ **6.** Which of these pictures illustrates why the summit in Paris did not take place?

a. Space Shuttle United States

b.

c.

d.

CHAPTER 19 The Cold War

MAIN IDEA ACTIVITIES 19.4

▰ VOCABULARY

Some terms to understand:

- **infiltrating (851):** entering or becoming established in gradually
- **malice (852):** ill will; spite
- **notorious (852):** widely and unfavorably known
- **alleged (854):** accused but not proven or convicted
- **atheism (856):** lack of a belief in God

▰ ORGANIZING INFORMATION Complete the chart about responses to the fear of communism in the United States, using the following items.

- House Un-American Activities Committee (HUAC)
- Internal Security Act
- Loyalty Review Board
- Religion

Responses to the Fear of Communism in the United States

1. _____	investigated all federal employees
2. _____	investigated communist groups in the United States
3. _____	required party members and organizations to register with the federal government
4. _____	gave many Americans a source of comfort from the fear of nuclear war

■ REVIEWING FACTS Choose the correct items from the following list to complete the statements below.

National Defense Administration   Central Intelligence Agency   air-raid drills
National Security Council   Joseph McCarthy   Alger Hiss
Julius and Ethel Rosenberg   Hollywood Ten
Sputnik   *Explorer I*

1. The _____ was established to advise the president on strategic matters.

2. The _____ was established to gather strategic military and political information overseas.

3. A group of actors known as the _____ refused to answer questions from the HUAC and were sent to jail.

4. _____ was a communist spy who hid the famous "pumpkin papers."

5. _____ were executed for supplying the Soviets with atomic energy secrets during World War II.

6. _____ claimed to have a list of Communists who worked at the State Department. He led a battle to remove Communists from the United States and was condemned by the Senate for conduct unbecoming a senator.

7. Schoolchildren went through _____ in which they crawled under their desks to protect themselves from radiation.

8. In October 1957 the Soviet Union launched the satellite _____.

9. In 1958 the United States sent the first U.S. satellite, _____, into orbit.

10. The _____ appropriated millions of dollars to improve education in science, mathematics, and foreign languages.

CHAPTER 20 Society After World War II

MAIN IDEA ACTIVITIES 20.1

■ VOCABULARY

Some terms to understand:

- **discharged (592):** released; let go
- **spurred (594):** pushed; urged
- **lynchings (594):** executions conducted without due process of law, usually by hanging
- **platform (596):** formal statement of principles and beliefs

■ ORGANIZING INFORMATION Complete the graphic organizer by filling in the appropriate bubbles with the following items.

- Progressive Party
- called for the repeal of the Taft-Hartley Act; an increase in federal aid for agriculture, education, and housing; broader Social Security benefits; and civil rights
- States' Rights Party (Dixiecrats)
- called for an extension of the New Deal and improved relations with the Soviet Union
- called for continued racial segregation

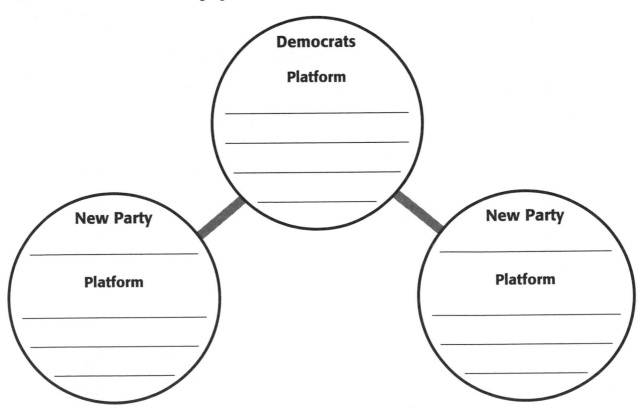

■ EVALUATING INFORMATION Mark each statement *T* if it is true or *F* if it is false.

_____ **1.** The GI Bill of Rights provided pensions and government loans to help veterans start businesses and buy homes or farms.

_____ **2.** The GI Bill of Rights was created to prevent an economic depression and help veterans make the transition back to civilian life.

_____ **3.** The Employment Act of 1946 stated that any veteran applying for a job must be hired.

_____ **4.** The Council of Economic Advisers was set up to work with the president on economic policy.

_____ **5.** After World War II U.S. food exports decreased.

_____ **6.** After wartime price controls were lifted in 1946, the cost of goods increased dramatically.

_____ **7.** There were many labor strikes after World War II, as workers tried to win wage increases and preserve price controls.

_____ **8.** President Truman supported the labor strikes saying they were good for the economy.

_____ **9.** When 400,000 coal miners went on strike, Truman ordered the army to take control of the mines.

_____ **10.** Truman threatened to end a railway strike by putting the strikers in jail.

_____ **11.** The Taft-Hartley Act reduced the strength of organized labor.

_____ **12.** President Truman vetoed the Taft-Hartley Act, but Congress overrode his veto.

_____ **13.** Truman created the Committee on Civil Rights to examine racism in the United States.

_____ **14.** Truman banned racial discrimination in the military and in federal hiring.

Main Idea Activities

CHAPTER 20

Society After World War II

MAIN IDEA ACTIVITIES 20.2

VOCABULARY

Some terms to understand:

• **bureaucracy (598):** running the government with the use of bureaus and procedures

• **curb (598):** limit; control

CLASSIFYING INFORMATION Mark these jobs as *B* (blue-collar), *W* (white-collar), or *P* (pink-collar).

_____ **1.** manager

_____ **2.** manufacturing jobs

_____ **3.** nursing

_____ **4.** teaching

_____ **5.** supervisors

_____ **6.** retail sales

EVALUATING INFORMATION Mark each statement *T* if it is true or *F* if it is false.

_____ **1.** President Eisenhower was determined to boost the economy and reform the federal government.

_____ **2.** In his first year as president, Eisenhower cut thousands of government jobs and billions of dollars from the federal budget.

_____ **3.** The 1950s was a decade of hard times for most Americans.

_____ **4.** Membership in labor unions declined during the 1950s.

_____ **5.** After World War II, Americans began to get married at younger ages and have more children.

_____ **6.** The number of working mothers increased during the 1950s.

_____ **7.** The teenagers' role changed in the 1950s because they no longer had to contribute to the family income.

■ UNDERSTANDING MAIN IDEAS For each of the following, write the letter of the *best* choice in the space provided.

_____ 1. Throughout the 1950s, companies introduced machines that could perform faster and more efficiently than human workers. This was called
    a. automation.
    b. machine technology.
    c. factory performance.
    d. production efficiency.

_____ 2. Pink-collar jobs were jobs filled by
    a. men.
    b. women.
    c. children.
    d. minorities.

_____ 3. To help workers improve their economic positions, union leaders
    a. raised wages.
    b. outlawed strikes.
    c. tried to cooperate with management.
    d. cut hours.

_____ 4. Which of these was not a component of the Landrum-Griffin Act?
    a. outlawed strikes
    b. banned ex-convicts from holding union offices
    c. required frequent elections of union officers
    d. regulated the investment of union funds

_____ 5. Which of these did not contribute to suburban growth in the 1950s?
    a. Housing costs were low.
    b. The population increased.
    c. The Highway Act made it easier for people to commute to jobs.
    d. Apartments in the city were overcrowded.

_____ 6. Which of these things had the most influence on advertising?

    a.

    b.

    c.

    d.

CHAPTER 20

Society After World War II

MAIN IDEA ACTIVITIES 20.3

■ VOCABULARY

Some terms to understand:

• **waged (607):** engaged in

• **boycott (610):** to quit buying, using, or doing something as a form of protest

• **urban areas (612):** cities

■ ORGANIZING INFORMATION Complete the chart below that explains how each person influenced the civil rights movement, using the following items.

• argued against school segregation before the Supreme Court

• a great leader for civil rights

• urged people to fight back peacefully

• refused to give up her seat to a white person; this led to the Montgomery Bus Boycott

• spokesperson for the Montgomery Improvement Association

Contributions to the Civil Rights Movement	
Thurgood Marshall	• _____ _____ _____
Rosa Parks	• _____ _____ _____
Martin Luther King Jr.	• _____ _____ • _____ _____ • _____ _____

■ **UNDERSTANDING MAIN IDEAS** For each of the following, write the letter of
the *best* choice in the space provided.

_____ 1. This Supreme Court case established the legality of "separate but
equal" educational facilities.
a. *Brown* v. *Board of Education*
b. *Plessy* v. *Ferguson*
c. *Méndez et al.* v. *Westminster
School District et al.*
d. *Delgado* v. *Bastrop Independent
School District*

_____ 2. This Supreme Court case ruling
declared segregation illegal in
public education.
a. *Brown* v. *Board of Education*
b. *Plessy* v. *Ferguson*
c. *Méndez et al.* v. *Westminster
School District et al.*
d. *Delgado* v. *Bastrop Independent
School District*

_____ 3. Who tried to interfere with Little
Rock's school desegregation plan?
a. Elizabeth Eckford
b. James F. Byrnes
c. Orval Faubus
d. President Eisenhower

_____ 4. Who was the spokesperson for
the Montgomery Improvement
Association?
a. Rosa Parks
b. President Eisenhower
c. President Truman
d. Martin Luther King Jr.

_____ 5. The _____ of 1957 made it a
federal crime to prevent qualified
persons from voting.
a. Montgomery Improvement
Association
b. League of United Latin
American Citizens
c. Voting Act
d. Civil Rights Act

_____ 6. Which of these events was a
major turning point for the civil
rights movement as it proved
minorities could stand up to people in positions of power?
a. *Plessy* v. *Ferguson*
b. March on Washington
c. Relocation of American
Indians
d. Montgomery bus boycott

_____ 7. The funeral home in Three
Rivers, Texas, refused to handle
Félix Longoria's burial because
a. he was black.
b. he was a Mexican American.
c. he had died during the war.
d. he did not pay his debts.

_____ 8. This Supreme Court case ruled
that the segregation of Mexican
American children in a Texas
school district was illegal.
a. *Brown* v. *Board of Education*
b. *Plessy* v. *Ferguson*
c. *Méndez et al.* v. *Westminster
School District et al.*
d. *Delgado* v. *Bastrop Independent
School District*

_____ 9. The Relocation Act of 1956 set up
procedures to encourage
American Indians to
a. stay on the reservations.
b. run for government offices.
c. marry outside their race.
d. move to urban areas.

The New Frontier and the Great Society

MAIN IDEA ACTIVITIES 21.1

■ VOCABULARY

An expression to understand:

- **pinned down (627):** conquered; stopped

Other terms:

- **implicit (624):** understood; having no doubt of
- **brief (624):** short

■ ORGANIZING INFORMATION Complete the chart about John F. Kennedy and Richard Nixon during the 1960 campaign, using the following items.

- selected Lyndon B. Johnson as his running mate
- Roman Catholic
- Eisenhower's vice president
- Republican
- Democrat
- voters were impressed by his record of service during World War II
- chose Henry Cabot Lodge Jr. as his running mate
- felt he had the maturity and experience to serve as president

1960 Campaign

Kennedy	Nixon
• _____	• _____
• _____	• _____
• _____	• _____
• _____	• _____

■ **REVIEWING FACTS** **Choose the correct item from the following list to complete the statements below.**

Peace Corps   Twenty-second Amendment   Texas
Nikita Khrushchev   Fidel Castro   Latin America
Bay of Pigs   flexible response   John F. Kennedy
television   African nations   developing countries
Berlin Wall   Limited Nuclear Test Ban Treaty

1. The _____ limited a president's time in office to two elected terms.

2. Kennedy felt that Johnson could help him win votes in _____.

3. During the Kennedy-Nixon debates, Nixon spoke well, and may have been considered the winner if he had not been seen on _____.

4. _____ was the youngest person ever elected to the White House.

5. Kennedy's strategy to have a number of options available during an international crisis was called _____.

6. Kennedy believed that helping _____ could strengthen their dependence on the United States and block Soviet influence.

7. The _____ was established to send American volunteers to work for two years in developing countries.

8. In 1960, when _____ received their independence from colonial powers, Kennedy called for an increase in economic aid to the continent.

9. The Alliance for Progress offered billions of dollars in aid to _____.

10. In 1959 _____ established a communist-style dictatorship in Cuba.

11. The U.S. invasion of Cuba at the _____ failed to overthrow Castro because Kennedy did not send air and naval support that the troops were expecting.

12. In June 1961 Soviet leader _____ ordered the West to recognize the sovereignty of communist East Germany and remove all troops from West Berlin.

13. The East Germans erected a barbed-wire barrier between East and West Berlin that eventually was rebuilt of concrete and called the _____.

14. In 1963 the United States, the Soviet Union, and Great Britain signed the _____ to end the testing of nuclear bombs in the atmosphere and underwater.

The New Frontier and the Great Society

MAIN IDEA ACTIVITIES 21.2

■ VOCABULARY

An expression to understand:

• **upset the applecart (634):** ruin the way things are

Other terms:

• **affluent (636):** well off; rich

• **profound (636):** of great depth; important

• **fatally wounded (636):** dead from a wound such as a gunshot

■ ORGANIZING INFORMATION Complete the chart about the Kennedy family, using the following items.

• brought an appreciation of the fine arts to the Kennedy administration

• graduate of Harvard University

• published two books

• organized a major restoration of the White House

• won a Pulitzer Prize

• the youngest to live in the White House since Theodore Roosevelt's presidency

• served as commander of a U.S. Navy patrol torpedo boat

• suffered from Addison's disease

John F. Kennedy	Jacqueline Kennedy	Kennedy Children
• _____	• _____	• _____
• _____	• _____	
• _____		
• _____		
• _____		

■ EVALUATING INFORMATION Mark each statement *T* if it is true or *F* if it is false.

_____ **1.** Most of Kennedy's cabinet members were younger than that of other presidents.

_____ **2.** It did not matter to Kennedy if his advisers came from great educational backgrounds or fine schools.

_____ **3.** Most of Kennedy's advisers were well experienced in politics and government affairs.

_____ **4.** Kennedy selected his brother, Robert Kennedy, to serve as attorney general.

_____ **5.** Kennedy's uncle was his closest adviser.

_____ **6.** Kennedy's political agenda was known as the New Frontier.

_____ **7.** Kennedy called for an increase in government spending to stimulate economic growth.

_____ **8.** Kennedy worked well with Congress and passed a great deal of legislation.

_____ **9.** President Kennedy donated his annual salary to charities.

_____ **10.** Kennedy's first legislative victory was the passage of the Area Redevelopment Act, which provided financial assistance to the poor.

_____ **11.** Kennedy was shot in Chicago where he had gone to build support for his 1964 presidential campaign.

_____ **12.** Lee Harvey Oswald killed President Kennedy.

The New Frontier and the Great Society

MAIN IDEA ACTIVITIES 21.3

■ VOCABULARY

Some terms to understand:

• **garbled (638):** hard to understand; distorted

• **transition (638):** change; adjustment to a new situation

• **advance (640):** put forward

• **liberal (640):** person who favors progress and reform, believes in freedom of individuals to act and express themselves as they choose, and is tolerant of new ideas and tend to give freely

■ ORGANIZING INFORMATION Complete the chart about the efforts that President Johnson made to carry out President Kennedy's War on Poverty by listing five programs he promoted.

The War on Poverty
• _____
• _____
• _____
• _____
• _____

■ EVALUATING INFORMATION Mark each statement *T* if it is true or *F* if it is false.

_____ **1.** President Johnson felt that women and minorities did not belong in government positions.

_____ **2.** Johnson's dream of a Great Society was "a place where all people would be more concerned with the quality of their goals than the quantity of their goods."

_____ **3.** President Johnson appointed Robert C. Weaver as head of the Department of Housing and Urban Development, making him the first African American member of a presidential cabinet.

_____ **4.** President Johnson was the only president in history who did not care about environmental issues.

_____ **5.** President Johnson was more interested in domestic policy than foreign affairs.

_____ **6.** In 1965 Johnson sent 22,000 marines to the Dominican Republic to quell the threat of communist expansion.

■ **UNDERSTANDING MAIN IDEAS** For each of the following, write the letter of the *best* choice in the space provided.

_____ **1.** Which of these antipoverty programs was a work training program for young people between the ages of 16 and 21?
   a. Job Corps
   b. Head Start
   c. VISTA
   d. Medicare

_____ **2.** Which of these antipoverty programs was a preschool education program for low income families?
   a. VISTA
   b. Head Start
   c. Medicare
   d. Job Corps

_____ **3.** Medicare was a national health insurance program for
   a. families with young children.
   b. people over age 65.
   c. criminals serving time in prison.
   d. veterans.

_____ **4.** Medicaid provided free health care to
   a. the seriously ill.
   b. veterans.
   c. minorities.
   d. the needy.

_____ **5.** The Elementary and Secondary Education Act of 1965
   a. provided $1.3 billion in aid to schools in impoverished areas.
   b. stated all children must graduate from high school.
   c. mandated that all towns with a population of 5,000 or more have both an elementary and secondary school.
   d. desegregated all of the nation's schools.

_____ **6.** The National Endowment for the Arts and the National Endowment for the Humanities offered grants and fellowships to artists, writers, and
   a. politicians.
   b. engineers.
   c. miners.
   d. scholars.

_____ **7.** Which Supreme Court case declared that all states must provide lawyers, at public expense, for impoverished defendants?
   a. *Baker* v. *Carr*
   b. *Gideon* v. *Wainwright*
   c. *Escobedo* v. *Illinois*
   d. *Miranda* v. *Arizona*

_____ **8.** Which Supreme Court case granted the accused the right to have a lawyer present during police investigations?
   a. *Baker* v. *Carr*
   b. *Gideon* v. *Wainwright*
   c. *Escobedo* v. *Illinois*
   d. *Miranda* v. *Arizona*

CHAPTER
22

The Civil Rights Movement

MAIN IDEA ACTIVITIES 22.1

◼ VOCABULARY

Some terms to understand:

• **vowing (650):** promising

• **nightsticks (654):** clubs carried by police officers

• **stalled (655):** made no progress

◼ CLASSIFYING INFORMATION Mark each statement with either *A* (Albany, Georgia) or *B* (Birmingham, Alabama) referring to the place where the civil rights activity occurred.

_____ **1.** Schoolchildren participated in the demonstrations.

_____ **2.** This march increased support for the civil rights movement.

_____ **3.** Police chief Laurie Pritchett quietly arrested the protesters.

_____ **4.** Martin Luther King Jr. was arrested and jailed.

_____ **5.** The police attacked marchers with dogs, fire hoses, and nightsticks.

_____ **6.** The media covered the protests.

_____ **7.** Bull Connor favored the use of violence to thwart the protests.

_____ **8.** This march taught the SCLC that civil rights progress only came when racists responded to peaceful demonstrations with violence.

◼ EVALUATING INFORMATION Mark each statement *T* if it is true or *F* if it is false.

_____ **1.** The Southern Christian Leadership Conference (SCLC) was a group of African American church-based organizations dedicated to ending discrimination.

_____ **2.** Nonviolent resistance allowed protesters to use violence only if they were being attacked.

_____ **3.** One of the ways African Americans protested discrimination at public lunch counters was to dump their food all over the counter.

_____ **4.** Sit-ins allowed protesters and city officials to sit down together and negotiate issues.

_____ **5.** The Student Nonviolent Coordinating Committee was an association of student activists from throughout the South.

_____ 6. When an angry mob beat nonviolent demonstrators in Nashville, Tennessee, the police arrested members of the mob.

_____ 7. The Freedom Riders were an integrated group of activists who planned to ride buses throughout the southern states.

_____ 8. The Freedom Riders were welcomed by supporters in Anniston, Alabama.

_____ 9. In Birmingham, Alabama, the Freedom Riders were viciously attacked and received no help from the police.

_____ 10. After numerous attacks, the Freedom Riders finally gave up.

_____ 11. James Meredith was the first African American to attend and graduate from the University of Mississippi.

■ INTERPRETING VISUAL IMAGES Examine the picture below and answer the questions that follow.

1. Drawing upon what you have read, where did this incident take place?

   _____

2. What action in this illustration alarmed people at the time?

   _____

3. Which public figure was forced to take a stand on civil rights after a photo of this action was published?

   _____

CHAPTER 22 The Civil Rights Movement

MAIN IDEA ACTIVITIES 22.2

■ VOCABULARY

A term to understand:

• **bigotry (660):** being intolerant of those who are different

■ ORGANIZING INFORMATION Complete the chart about organizations and legislation promoting black voter registration in the South, using the following items.

• provided money from private foundations to fund registration projects

• enlisted white volunteers from northern universities to help with registration projects

• placed the registration process under federal control

• organized registration of black voters in the South

• conducted two mock elections to introduce voting procedures to African Americans

SNCC	• _____ _____
Voter Education Project	• _____ _____
COFO	• _____ _____
Freedom Summer	• _____ _____
Voting Rights Act of 1965	• _____ _____

▓▓ UNDERSTANDING MAIN IDEAS For each of the following, write the letter of the *best* choice in the space provided.

_____ 1. Which of these was not a means
to prevent African Americans
from registering to vote?
   a. literacy tests
   b. violence
   c. bribes of money
   d. fear of loss of employment

_____ 2. Which state where racial violence
had occurred was chosen to be
the first voter registration project?
   a. Missouri
   b. Mississippi
   c. Texas
   d. Georgia

_____ 3. Who suggested bringing in white
volunteers to help with the voter
registration projects?
   a. Andrew Goodman
   b. James Chaney
   c. Michael Schwemer
   d. Robert Moses

_____ 4. James Chaney, Michael
Schwemer, and _____ were volunteers during Freedom Summer
who were killed for their efforts.
   a. Andrew Goodman
   b. James Chaney
   c. Michael Schwemer
   d. Robert Moses

_____ 5. By the end of Freedom Summer,
_____ African American voters
had been added to the voting
rolls.
   a. 16
   b. 160
   c. 1,600
   d. 16,000

_____ 6. Which of these people was an
MFDP delegate who lost her job
and her home when she regis-
tered to vote?
   a. Fannie Lou Hamer
   b. Victoria Taylor
   c. Sojouner Truth
   d. Rosa Parks

_____ 7. In which city of Alabama did the
registration of African American
voters turn into "Bloody
Sunday"?
   a. Montgomery
   b. Birmingham
   c. Albany
   d. Selma

The Civil Rights Movement

MAIN IDEA ACTIVITIES 22.3

■ VOCABULARY

Some terms to understand:

• **confrontational (661):** defiant; hostile

• **spawned (661):** produced

• **championed (662):** became a force for

• **perceived (663):** saw; thought of in a certain way

■ EVALUATING INFORMATION Mark each statement *T* if it is true or *F* if it is false.

_____ **1.** As the civil rights movement continued, some African Americans questioned the effectiveness of nonviolence as a mean to reach their goals.

_____ **2.** The Black Muslims emphasized the supremacy of black people over all other races.

_____ **3.** Elijah Muhammad declared that African Americans should create their own republic within the United States.

_____ **4.** Black Muslims received great financial aid from the federal government.

_____ **5.** Malcolm X embraced the teachings of Elijah Muhammad and became a leading minister for the Nation of Islam.

_____ **6.** Malcolm X criticized the goals and strategies of civil rights organizations.

_____ **7.** Malcolm X was assassinated by Black Muslim members.

_____ **8.** In 1966 Martin Luther King Jr. moved his family into a slum apartment in Chicago because he had used up all of his money funding the civil rights movement.

_____ **9.** African Americans received great support from whites in their fight for civil rights in the North.

_____ **10.** In 1968 Martin Luther King Jr. called for a Poor People's Campaign that would include a march on Washington to protest the misuse of government spending.

_____ **11.** On April 4, 1968, Martin Luther King Jr. was assassinated in Memphis, Tennessee.

■ UNDERSTANDING MAIN IDEAS For each of the following, write the letter of the *best* choice in the space provided.

_____ 1. Who became the leader of the Black Muslims in the early 1930s?
   a. Huey Newton
   b. Bobby Seale
   c. Elijah Muhammad
   d. Malcolm X

_____ 2. Which of these was not an expectation of Black Muslim members?
   a. no alcohol
   b. no smoking
   c. maintain membership in the armed forces
   d. maintain a strict diet

_____ 3. During World War II many Black Muslims were sent to prison for
   a. spying.
   b. burglary.
   c. murder.
   d. avoiding the draft.

_____ 4. When the Nation of Islam's membership declined, Muhammad began actively recruiting
   a. Catholics.
   b. women.
   c. convicts.
   d. Mexican Americans.

_____ 5. Malcolm X converted to _____ and began calling for unity among all people.
   a. Islam
   b. Catholicism
   c. Buddhism
   d. Judaism

_____ 6. The presence of white volunteers created tensions within the SNCC because African American workers believed that white students were
   a. spying on them for government officials.
   b. doing their jobs incorrectly.
   c. trying to stop the civil rights movement.
   d. trying to take over the project.

_____ 7. Which of these was not a premise of the Black Power movement?
   a. black separatism
   b. emphasis on racial pride
   c. interest in African culture and heritage
   d. abolishment of slavery around the world

_____ 8. Which of these became the symbol of a militant black party?

   a.   c.

   b.   d.

_____ 9. The Kerner Commission charged that _____ was largely responsible for the riots of 1965 and 1966.
   a. white racism
   b. African American
   c. poverty
   d. Black Power

The Civil Rights Movement

MAIN IDEA ACTIVITIES 22.4

■ VOCABULARY

Some terms to understand:

• **assassination (667):** murder

• **dissented (669):** disagreed

■ ORGANIZING INFORMATION Complete the chart by writing five problems many civil rights organizations encountered in the early 1970s.

Problems of Civil Rights Organizations
• _____ _____
• _____ _____
• _____ _____
• _____ _____
• _____ _____

■ EVALUATING INFORMATION Mark each statement *T* if it is true or *F* if it is false.

_____ **1.** Resurrection City was created to draw attention to African American poverty.

_____ **2.** Resurrection City was a great success for the civil rights movement.

_____ **3.** Some school districts bused children to schools outside of their neighborhoods to protect them from racial violence.

Main Idea Activities

Chapter 22 **155**

_____ **4.** Most white Americans opposed busing.

_____ **5.** Many white critics of affirmative action argued that its programs led to "reverse dis-crimination."

_____ **6.** During the 1970s African Americans made no advances in the civil rights move-ment.

_____ **7.** The National Black Political Convention was formed to ensure that African Americans would continue to gain political influence.

▮▮REVIEWING FACTS Choose the correct items from the following list to complete the statements below.

University of California v. *Bakke*	quota
Milliken v. *Bradley*	Carl Stokes
Griggs v. *Duke Power Company*	affirmative action

1. The Supreme Court case _____ merged Detroit's inner-city school districts with the city's suburban districts.

2. _____ programs gave preference to ethnic minorities and women in admission and hiring.

3. The Supreme Court case _____ ruled that in the future, compa-nies would have to explain why tests for advancement were necessary.

4. A _____ is a fixed number of openings for a certain group of people.

5. The Supreme Court case _____ ruled that a white man had been unfairly denied admission to a medical school on the basis of quotas.

6. _____ was the first African American to be elected mayor of Cleveland.

CHAPTER 23

Struggles for Change

MAIN IDEA ACTIVITIES 23.1

■ VOCABULARY

Some terms to understand:

• **feminists (679):** women who demand the same rights for women as are granted to men

• **primarily (680):** for the most part

■ ORGANIZING INFORMATION Complete the chart below by listing four ways the federal government helped the women's cause.

Federal Government's Aid to Women
• _____   _____
• _____   _____
• _____   _____
• _____   _____

▧ EVALUATING INFORMATION Mark each statement *T* if it is true and *F* if it is false.

_____ 1. Author Betty Friedan sparked a revival in the women's movement with her book *The Feminine Mystique.*

_____ 2. During Friedan's survey of women, she concluded that many found full-time home-making unfulfilling.

_____ 3. In 1960 men and women received equal pay for equal work.

_____ 4. The Kennedy administration hired many women.

_____ 5. Title VII of the Civil Rights Act of 1964 outlawed sexual discrimination in employment.

_____ 6. The National Organization for Women (NOW) was created to pressure elected officials to ensure social and economic equality for women.

_____ 7. In 1968 feminists stated that beauty pageants worked toward women's rights by putting women in the media.

_____ 8. Gloria Steinem founded the National Women's Political Caucus to encourage women to run for political office.

_____ 9. The Education Amendments Act outlawed sexual discrimination in higher education.

_____ 10. In the Supreme Court case *Roe* v. *Wade,* the Court ruled that the state should not make decisions regarding a woman's right to receive an abortion.

_____ 11. Opponents of *Roe* v. *Wade* protested that the ruling violated the rights of the father.

_____ 12. Bella Abzug and Shirley Chisholm were both New York representatives.

_____ 13. During the 1970s the number of women holding professional jobs decreased.

CHAPTER 23 Struggles for Change

MAIN IDEA ACTIVITIES 23.2

VOCABULARY

Some terms to understand:

- **consumers (683):** people who buy goods
- **fraud (684):** deception; cheating
- **entangled (684):** tied up
- **disenchanted (686):** disappointed

CLASSIFIYING INFORMATION Mark each action of the Chicano Movement with *C* (Chávez) for César Chávez , *T* (Tijerina) for Reijes Lopez Tijerina, or *G* (Gonzales) for Rodolfo Gonzales.

_____ **1.** founded the National Farm Workers Association (NFWA)

_____ **2.** founded the Crusade for Justice, a group that promoted Mexican American nationalism

_____ **3.** popularized the term "Chicano" to refer to Mexican Americans

_____ **4.** conducted a 300-mile march to Sacramento, California

_____ **5.** tried to regain land that Mexican Americans had lost

_____ **6.** called for a nationwide boycott of grapes

_____ **7.** did not achieve his goals, but did inspire others to take militant action

EVALUATING INFORMATION Mark each statement *T* if it is true or *F* if it is false.

_____ **1.** The Mexican American struggle to secure equal rights was not very powerful.

_____ **2.** In the 1960s Mexican Americans were some of the richest and best educated people in the country.

_____ **3.** U.S. consumers did not respond to the boycott of grapes and the protest failed.

_____ **4.** The United Farm Workers was formed by the merging of the NFWA with another union.

_____ **5.** Many Mexican Americans in East Los Angeles were upset with the poor quality of the local schools.

_____ **6.** The Educational Issues Coordinating Committee (EICC) used violent tactics to try to bring about change in the school system.

_____ **7.** The East Los Angeles school walkouts brought national attention to Mexican American concerns and drew many students into militant activism.

_____ **8.** Gutiérrez and other MAYO leaders held a student walkout that forced the Crystal City school board to end discrimination in extracurricular activities.

■ UNDERSTANDING MAIN IDEAS For each of the following, write the letter of the *best* choice in the space provided.

_____ **1.** After NFWA members voted to strike, which of these things was not an action taken by Chávez?
  a. collected donations of money and food
  b. opened a school
  c. opened a medical clinic
  d. operated a gas station

_____ **2.** Which of these symbolized the Mexican American rights movement?

  a.   **c.**

  b.   **d.**

_____ **3.** Which of these was not a service of the Crusade for Justice?
  a. operated a school
  b. offered legal aid
  c. operated a theater
  d. funded Mexican American housing

_____ **4.** The _____ were an activist group that opposed police brutality against Mexican Americans.
  a. Brown Berets
  b. Green Berets
  c. Blackshirts
  d. Brownshirts

_____ **5.** *Aliancistas* referred to
  a. followers of Chávez.
  b. followers of Tijerina.
  c. followers of Gonzales.
  d. followers of Gutiérrez.

_____ **6.** *El Plan Espiritual de Aztlán*, or *The Spiritual Plan of Aztlán*, called for
  a. civil war.
  b. peace between Chicanos and African Americans.
  c. Chicano separatism.
  d. Catholicism as the national religion.

_____ **7.** La Raza Unida Party (RUP) gained control of the city council in
  a. Crystal City.
  b. Dallas.
  c. Sacramento.
  d. Albany.

_____ **8.** Which of these was *not* a victory of the Chicano movement?
  a. several universities established Chicano Studies programs
  b. inspired Mexican American artists, novelists, and playwrights to create new works
  c. activists entered mainstream politics
  d. Mexican Americans regained all of their lost lands

CHAPTER 23

Struggles for Change

MAIN IDEA ACTIVITIES 23.3

■ VOCABULARY

Some terms to understand:

- **siege (690):** surrounding, blocking, or occupying of an area by force
- **quadriplegic (691):** someone who is paralyzed from the neck down

- **braille (691):** system of writing and printing for the blind that uses raised dots for the letters of the alphabet
- **eradicate (693):** get rid of

■ ORGANIZING INFORMATION Complete the chart about American Indians, using the following items.

- recover land in over half the state that had been taken from them
- recover 48,000 acres of land that was sacred to the tribe
- authorities removed protesters from the island
- wanted renewal of American Indian culture and recognition of American Indian rights

- their land was returned
- the government agreed to consider AIM's grievances
- were awarded $81.5 million and the right to buy up to 300,000 acres of land
- occupied Alcatraz and offered to buy the island for the same price as was paid for Manhattan Island

Group or Event	Goal	Outcome
American Indians of All Tribes		
Wounded Knee		
Taos Pueblo		
American Indians in Maine		

▚ REVIEWING FACTS Choose the correct item from the following list to complete the statements below.

Education for All Handicapped Children Act   Gray Panthers
Ed Roberts   Maggie Kuhn
Children's Bill of Rights   poverty
Rolling Quads   self-determination
American Association of Retired Persons   Rehabilitation Act
Older Americans Act

1. American Indians were particularly affected by _____.

2. The Red Power movement called for _____, or the right to govern their own communities.

3. _____ was a quadriplegic who wanted people with physical disabilities to have access to public facilities.

4. The _____ was a support group for students with disabilities at Berkeley.

5. In 1973 Congress passed the _____, which forbade discrimination in education, housing, or jobs because of physical disabilities.

6. The _____ required public schools to provide education for children with physical or mental disabilities.

7. The _____ was the largest group to lobby for the needs of older citizens.

8. The _____ was a highly visible group who worked for the senior movement.

9. _____ was the founder of the Gray Panthers.

10. In 1965 Congress passed the _____, which committed the government to provide the elderly with adequate income and medical care.

11. The _____ declared that children had the "right to grow in a society which respects the dignity of life and is free of poverty, discrimination, and other forms of degradation."

CHAPTER 23 **Struggles for Change**

MAIN IDEA ACTIVITIES 23.4

■ VOCABULARY

Some terms to understand:

- **tube (694):** television
- **communes (695):** small communities whose members share common interests
- **sinister characters (696):** evil people
- **irrelevant (696):** pointless
- **soundtrack (698):** music

■ ORGANIZING INFORMATION Complete the graphic organizer below by listing six things that describe the fashion of the counterculture.

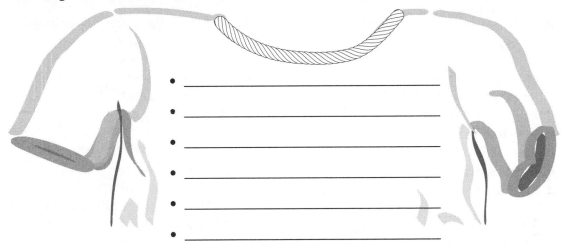

■ EVALUATING INFORMATION Mark each statement *T* if it is true or *F* if it is false.

_____ 1. A large number of Berkeley students stopped attending classes and held demonstrations when officials announced a new policy restricting space available to students for making speeches.

_____ 2. Hippies were in favor of a simpler lifestyle and supported "doing your own thing."

_____ 3. In the 1960s the number of college courses in religion declined.

_____ 4. Pop art was a new style of art intended to appeal to popular tastes in society.

_____ 5. In the 1960s folk music gained popularity once again.

_____ 6. Berry Gordy founded Motown Records, which banned African Americans from the music business.

_____ 7. Woodstock was a rock concert that marked the high point of the counterculture movement.

■ UNDERSTANDING MAIN IDEAS For each of the following, write the letter of the *best* choice in the space provided.

_____ 1. During the 1960s many young people began to blame _____ for creating the problems that the country faced.
   a. the government
   b. their parents
   c. immigrants
   d. religion

_____ 2. The group of people who rejected everything connected with mainstream America were known as
   a. socialists.
   b. communists.
   c. nationalists.
   d. hippies.

_____ 3. Many hippies joined _____ where they attempted to live in harmony with nature.
   a. the army
   b. the convent
   c. communes
   d. the church

_____ 4. Who was fired from his job after using "acid" on college students?
   a. Timothy Leary
   b. Bob Dylan
   c. James Brown
   d. Charles Kaiser

_____ 5. Which of these was *NOT* a downfall of the counterculture?
   a. increase in drug addiction
   b. increase in sexually transmitted diseases
   c. living in harsh urban neighborhoods
   d. increased enrollment in religious courses

_____ 6. During the 1960s the film industry
   a. quit making family films.
   b. hired only hippies.
   c. was closed down due to unpopular films.
   d. adopted its film rating system.

_____ 7. Which of these artists did paintings in comic-strip style?
   a. Roy Lichtenstein
   b. Claes Oldenburg
   c. Andy Warhol
   d. Norman Rockwell

_____ 8. Which of these artists was known for mass-production in art?
   a. Roy Lichtenstein
   b. Claes Oldenburg
   c. Andy Warhol
   d. Norman Rockwell

_____ 9. The British invasion was
   a. Great Britain declaring war on the United States.
   b. the invasion of British immigrants in the United States.
   c. the introduction of British bands to the American audience.
   d. the introduction of British films to the United States.

_____ 10. Who brought folk music into the rock music realm?
   a. Joan Baez
   b. Bob Dylan
   c. Janis Joplin
   d. Rolling Stones

★ War in Vietnam

MAIN IDEA ACTIVITIES 24.1

■ VOCABULARY

Some terms to understand:

- **delta (706):** triangular deposit of soil at the mouth of a river
- **guerrilla warfare (706):** war fought by small groups of men using acts of harassment and sabotage
- **assert (710):** demonstrate in a forceful way

■ EVALUATING INFORMATION Mark each statement *T* if it is true or *F* if it is false.

_____ **1.** The Vietnamese people had been fighting to gain and protect their freedom and independence for more than 1,000 years.

_____ **2.** Vietnam is the westernmost country of Southeast Asia.

_____ **3.** The Mekong Delta is Vietnam's richest agricultural region, specializing in sugar cane production.

_____ **4.** In the 1800s Cambodia, Laos, and Vietnam were referred to as French Indochina.

■ ORGANIZING INFORMATION Complete the chart that explains why China and France wanted to control Vietnam, using the following items.

- because of its agricultural abundance
- for gaining access to Asian trade
- in order to make new Catholic converts

China	• _____
France	• _____
	• _____

■ UNDERSTANDING MAIN IDEAS For each of the following, write the letter of the *best* choice in the space provided.

_____ 1. Who plotted for Vietnamese independence during the 1920s and 1930s?
   a. Le Loi
   b. Ho Chi Minh
   c. Ngo Dinh Diem
   d. Trieu Au

_____ 2. What did Ho call his resistance movement?
   a. Vietminh
   b. Vietcong
   c. Domino Theory
   d. Indochina

_____ 3. Why did President Truman give U.S. support to France in its battle with Ho and his followers?
   a. Ho did not ask for America's help.
   b. Ho already had enough troops and supplies.
   c. France was a poorer, weaker nation.
   d. Truman viewed France as a vital ally in the struggle against communism.

_____ 4. The _____ stated that if Vietnam fell to communism, the rest of Southeast Asia would soon follow.
   a. domino theory
   b. communism theory
   c. Vietnam theory
   d. Southeast Asia theory

_____ 5. In 1963 _____ leaders began quietly encouraging a group of South Vietnamese army officers plotting Diem's overthrow.
   a. French
   b. Spanish
   c. Chinese
   d. United States

_____ 6. How did Ngo Dinh Diem become president of South Vietnam?
   a. He was crowned king.
   b. He overthrew the king.
   c. He was elected fairly.
   d. He was elected in a fixed election.

_____ 7. Which of these was not a reason that Diem was so unpopular as a president?
   a. He showed favoritism toward Catholics.
   b. He favored wealthy landholders.
   c. People feared his ruthless efforts to wipe out his enemies.
   d. He was a Buddhist.

_____ 8. The National Liberation Front's (NLF) main goal was to
   a. overthrow Ngo Dinh Diem.
   b. overthrow North Vietnam.
   c. run France out of Southeast Asia.
   d. reunite North and South Vietnam.

_____ 9. President Kennedy increased U.S. involvement in Vietnam because
   a. he wanted to do everything the opposite of President Truman.
   b. he wanted to have Vietnam for a U.S. territory.
   c. he wanted to assert U.S. power in the world.
   d. he wanted another world war.

_____ 10. Ho Chi Minh used _____ to defeat the French.
   a. tear gas
   b. atomic bombs
   c. air raids
   d. guerrilla warfare

CHAPTER 24 War in Vietnam

MAIN IDEA ACTIVITIES 24.2

■ VOCABULARY

An expression to understand:

- **booby traps (715):** hidden explosive devices

Other terms:

- **rice paddies (715):** area where rice is grown
- **petition (718):** formal written document requesting something

■ CLASSIFYING INFORMATION Complete the chart about the views of the doves and hawks toward the war in Vietnam, using the following items.

- opposed the war
- pacifists believed that war was wrong
- argued for more U.S. troops
- felt that the United States was fighting against the wishes of a majority of Vietnamese

- supported the war's goals
- felt that Vietnam was not crucial to national security
- wanted heavier bombing

Doves	Hawks
• _____	• _____
• _____	• _____
• _____	• _____
• _____	

■ EVALUATING INFORMATION Mark each statement *T* if it is true or *F* if it is false.

_____ **1.** In 1963 the U.S. Secretary of Defense was Robert S. McNamara.

_____ **2.** McNamara advised President Johnson not to give any more aid to Vietnam.

_____ **3.** By passing the Tonkin Gulf Resolution, Congress gave up its power to declare war.

_____ **4.** At the height of the war, the average U.S. soldier in Vietnam was less educated, poorer, and younger than those who had served in World War II.

_____ **5.** Very few African Americans or Hispanics served in the Vietnam War.

_____ **6.** The Ho Chi Minh Trail was a network of jungle paths used by the North Vietnamese to bring weapons and supplies into South Vietnam.

_____ **7.** Between 1965 and 1967 the number of U.S. troops in Vietnam decreased by about 300,000.

_____ **8.** During search-and-destroy missions, U.S. ground patrols located the enemy and then called in air support to attack them.

_____ **9.** The media had a positive impact on U.S. citizens' attitudes toward the war.

_____ **10.** Civil rights activists claimed that the U.S. government was sending African Americans off to war while doing little to end racism in the states.

■ REVIEWING FACTS Choose the correct items from the following list to complete the statements below.

college deferments	defoliants	10,000
Tonkin Gulf Resolution	whites	escalation
Operation Rolling Thunder	2 million	pacification
Agent Orange		

1. The _____ gave the president authority to take "all necessary measures to repel any armed attack against forces of the United States."

2. President Johnson called for a(n) _____, or build up, of U.S. military troops in Vietnam.

3. During the war more than _____ Americans served in Vietnam.

4. Young men from higher-income families were the least likely to be drafted because of

_____.

5. Some _____ women served in Vietnam.

6. _____ was a bombing campaign against military targets in North Vietnam.

7. _____ were chemicals sprayed by U.S. planes that stripped the land of vegetation.

8. The most widely used chemical during the Vietnam War was

_____.

9. _____ was the movement of village residents to refugee camps or cities so that the villages could be burnt.

10. Polls showed that blacks were much more likely than _____ to be opposed to the war.

War in Vietnam

CHAPTER 24

MAIN IDEA ACTIVITIES 24.3

■ VOCABULARY

Some terms to understand:

- **permeated (720):** penetrated; spread through
- **lull (720):** break
- **disperse (722):** break up
- **eradicate (724):** get rid of
- **endurance (725):** ability to withstand hardship

■ EVALUATING INFORMATION Mark each statement *T* if it is true or *F* if it is false.

_____ **1.** In 1968 the United States realized it was not winning the Vietnam War.

_____ **2.** The Tet Offensive was an attack by the North Vietnamese during the Vietnamese New Year, a holiday that had been previously honored by a lull in fighting.

_____ **3.** The Tet Offensive boosted America's confidence in winning the war.

_____ **4.** After the Tet Offensive, public criticism of the war rose dramatically.

_____ **5.** President Johnson announced that he would not seek re-election.

_____ **6.** Robert Kennedy would have been the Democrats' nominee for president, but he did not receive enough votes.

_____ **7.** Antiwar protesters held a protest outside of the Democratic convention in Chicago.

_____ **8.** The Chicago protesters were attacked by the police.

_____ **9.** The Republicans' nominee for president, Richard Nixon, told voters he had a plan to end the war.

_____ **10.** Richard Nixon lost the presidential race.

_____ **11.** President Nixon, aided by Henry Kissinger, made foreign affairs his top priority.

_____ **12.** Henry Kissinger won the Nobel Peace Prize for his role in negotiations that eventually ended the Vietnam War.

■ **ORGANIZING INFORMATION** Use the following items to complete the chart about Vietnamization.

• troop withdrawls began in August 1969

• to produce a stable anticommunist government

• to obtain peace with honor

• gradual withdrawal of troops over the next four years

Vietnamization

Reasons	Steps
• _____	• _____
• _____	• _____

■ **UNDERSTANDING MAIN IDEAS** For each of the following, write the letter of the *best* choice in the space provided.

_____ **1.** President Nixon secretly planned to expand the war into
a. Laos.
b. China.
c. France.
d. Cambodia.

_____ **2.** Early in 1969 Nixon ordered the widespread bombing of
a. Cambodia.
b. Laos.
c. France.
d. China.

_____ **3.** On May 4, 1970, National Guard troops sent in to control demonstrators at Kent State shot randomly into a large group of students, killing four and injuring nine others. This event was referred to as the
a. Kent State killings.
b. Kent State shootings.
c. Kent State massacre.
d. Kent State demonstration.

_____ **4.** The Pentagon Papers revealed that
a. the U.S. government was being run by Communists.
b. the United States really was winning the war.
c. the government had misled the American people about the course of the war.
d. the Pentagon would be shutting down the war.

_____ **5.** The invasion of Cambodia and the renewed bombing of North Vietnam
a. ended the war.
b. slowed down the war.
c. caused Americans to embrace the war.
d. caused Congress to repeal the Gulf of Tonkin Resolution.

War in Vietnam

MAIN IDEA ACTIVITIES 24.4

■ VOCABULARY

An expression to understand:

• **ticker-tape parade (729):** traditional hero's welcome in which ribbons are thrown from the tops of buildings while heroes parade by

Other term:

• **paranoiac (726):** without logic or reason

■ ORGANIZING INFORMATION Complete the chart describing George McGovern and Richard Nixon using the following items.

• voiced a strong commitment to law and order
• deeply opposed the war in Vietnam
• Air Force pilot in World War II
• assured voters that the war would soon be over
• senator from South Dakota

McGovern	Nixon
• _____	• _____
• _____	• _____
• _____	

■ EVALUATING INFORMATION Mark each statement *T* if it is true or *F* if it is false.

_____ **1.** Nixon won the 1972 presidential election by a very slim margin.

_____ **2.** The United States rejected the peace plan offered by the North Vietnamese in October 1972 because the United States supported the president of South Vietnam.

_____ **3.** The United States accepted the cease-fire of January 1973 because it allowed both sides to claim a diplomatic victory.

_____ **4.** Nixon pledged to never interfere in Vietnam again.

_____ **5.** America succeeded in preventing the creation of a united, independent Vietnam under communist rule.

■ REVIEWING FACTS Choose the correct item from the following list to complete the statements below.

2 million	Twenty-sixth Amendment	defoliants
Vietnam Veterans Memorial	1 million	birth defects
War Powers Act	East Meets West Foundation	

1. The _____ lowered the voting age from 21 to 18.

2. The number of Vietcong and North Vietnamese casualties during the Vietnam War is esti-

mated at _____.

3. Le Ly Hayslip founded the _____ to provide comfort to all the victims of war.

4. More than _____ Americans were involved in the Vietnam War.

5. Many soldiers who were involved with the spraying of

_____ developed cancer.

6. The children of veterans who had been exposed to Agent Orange had a high rate of

_____.

7. The _____ reaffirmed Congress's constitutional right to declare war by setting a 60-day limit on the presidential commitment of U.S. troops to foreign conflicts.

8. The _____ is a huge wall of black granite engraved with the names of more than 58,000 soldiers who died in Vietnam.

CHAPTER 25 — From Nixon to Carter

MAIN IDEA ACTIVITIES 25.1

■ VOCABULARY

Some terms to understand:

- **embargo (743):** when the government puts a stop on trading a particular item
- **emissions (744):** amount of pollution produced by a car or truck

■ ORGANIZING INFORMATION Complete the chart about President Nixon's actions, using the following items.

- appointed conservative judges to the Supreme Court
- temporarily froze wages, prices, and rents
- increased support for the use of nuclear energy
- reduced the highway speed limit to 55 miles per hour
- proposed the Family Assistance Plan
- authorized the construction of a pipeline to transport oil from Alaska
- delayed pressuring schools to desegregate

President Nixon's Actions

Welfare	• _____
Southern Support	• _____ • _____
Economy	• _____
Energy Crisis	• _____ • _____ • _____

■ REVIEWING FACTS Choose the correct items from the following list to complete the statements below.

Family Assisstance Plan
Clean Air Act
the People's Republic of China
Arab
Endangered Species Act
southern strategy
stagflation

Water Quality Improvement Act
middle-class
realpolitik
Environmental Protection Agency
détente
Organization of Petroleum Exporting Countries

1. Much of President Nixon's support came from _____ voters.

2. The _____ would guarantee families a minimum income.

3. President Nixon's plan to gain southern support was called his

   _____.

4. The combination of rising unemployment and inflation is called

   _____.

5. During the 1970s the cost of oil rose because several _____ nations cut off oil shipments to the United States.

6. The _____ was a group founded by several oil-producing countries to obtain higher oil prices.

7. The _____ was given the power to enforce environmental laws.

8. The _____ set air-quality standards and tough emissions guidelines for car manufacturers.

9. The _____ made oil companies pay some of the cleanup costs of oil spills.

10. The _____ was designed to protect animal species in danger of extinction.

11. Nixon's belief in emphasizing national interest over moral or ethical concerns was called

    _____.

12. President Nixon sought to improve relations with _____.

13. As a result of the Moscow Summit, the Soviet Union and the United States entered into a

    period of _____, or the lessening of military and diplomatic tensions between two countries.

CHAPTER 25

From Nixon to Carter

MAIN IDEA ACTIVITIES 25.2

■ VOCABULARY

Some expressions to understand:

- **held office by appointment (750):** they were not elected
- **"I'm a Ford, not a Lincoln." (751):** I'm plain, not fancy.

Other terms:

- **complied (749):** obeyed
- **clemency (751):** leniency
- **recession (752):** a decline in economic activity

■ ORGANIZING INFORMATION Complete the chart about public opinion regarding President Ford's actions, using the following items.

- Ford's popularity dropped
- unfair to soldiers who had served their country
- double standard
- was agreed upon in advance
- full truth about Watergate would never be known
- "We weren't criminals."

President Ford's Actions

Nixon's Pardon	Clemency for Vietnam Draft Evaders
• _____	• _____
• _____	• _____
• _____	
• _____	

▮▮ EVALUATING INFORMATION Mark each statement *T* if it is true or *F* if it is false.

_____ 1. In 1972 five men were caught breaking into the offices of the Democratic National Committee in the Watergate building in Washington, D.C.

_____ 2. Nixon's campaign organization had hired 50 agents to sabotage the Democrats' chances in the 1972 election.

_____ 3. Tape-recorded conversations in the White House proved that Nixon had nothing to do with the Watergate scandal.

_____ 4. Nixon quietly turned in the tapes after an order from the court.

_____ 5. Vice President Agnew was charged with tax evasion and resigned his post.

_____ 6. President Ford vetoed more bills during his term in office than any other president in the same amount of time.

_____ 7. President Ford secretly aided the National Front in Angola.

▮▮ REVIEWING FACTS Choose the correct items from the following list to complete the statements below.

Barbara Jordan	Sam Ervin	plumbers
inflation	Gerald Ford	*Mayaguez*

1. The _____ were a group ordered to stop leaks and carry out a variety of illegal actions during the Nixon administration.

2. _____ led the Senate investigation into the Watergate scandal.

3. _____ was the first African American woman elected to the Texas state senate.

4. _____ became vice president by appointment and became president when the previous president resigned.

5. One of President Ford's main goals was to combat _____.

6. President Ford launched a military action after Cambodian Communists seized the

_____, a U.S. cargo ship.

CHAPTER 25 From Nixon to Carter

MAIN IDEA ACTIVITIES 25.3

◼ VOCABULARY

An expression to understand:

• **curb inflation (755):** to stop or slow the inflation rate

◼ ORGANIZING INFORMATION Complete the chart by listing four things Jimmy Carter did and said as a candidate.

Candidate Jimmy Carter
• _____
_____
• _____
_____
• _____
_____
• _____
_____

◼ EVALUATING INFORMATION Mark each statement *T* if it is true or *F* if it is false.

_____ **1.** President Carter's approval rating dropped dramatically after his first 100 days in office.

_____ **2.** Carter's anti-inflation program slowed inflation and cut unemployment.

_____ **3.** The National Energy Act that Carter proposed was changed dramatically by Congress.

_____ **4.** After the Three Mile Island incident, President Carter called for the shutdown of all nuclear power plants.

_____ **5.** President Carter called for strong diplomatic pressure on countries that violated human rights.

_____ **6.** Relations with the Soviet Union improved during Carter's term.

_____ **7.** President Carter helped with the Camp David Accords, which set a framework for peace in the Middle East.

■ **UNDERSTANDING MAIN IDEAS** For each of the following, write the letter of the *best* choice in the space provided.

_____ 1. Who said, "I will never lie to you; I will never mislead you"?
   a. Gerald Ford
   b. Ronald Reagan
   c. Richard Nixon
   d. Jimmy Carter

_____ 2. What did President Carter's decision to walk to the White House on Inauguration Day symbolize?
   a. his efforts to save money
   b. his desire for physical fitness
   c. his desire to keep his administration open to public view
   d. his dislike of limousines

_____ 3. Which action did President Carter take to keep in touch with the American people?
   a. held town meetings
   b. raised taxes
   c. rode in a limousine
   d. captured electoral votes

_____ 4. In January 1979 OPEC
   a. lowered the price of oil by 50 percent.
   b. raised the price of oil by 50 percent.
   c. found new oil wells in Alaska.
   d. stopped sending oil to the United States.

_____ 5. The Panama Canal Treaties
   a. gave the U.S. permanent control over the Canal Zone.
   b. ended a war being fought in Panama.
   c. granted Panama immediate control over canal operations.
   d. granted Panama control over canal operations by the year 2000.

_____ 6. Which of these was *NOT* a cause of conflict with the Soviet Union?
   a. U.S. criticism of their human rights record
   b. improved relations between the United States and China
   c. the U.S. boycott of the 1980 Summer Olympics in Moscow
   d. the Middle East peace accord

From Nixon to Carter

MAIN IDEA ACTIVITIES 25.4

■ VOCABULARY

Some terms to understand:

• **commemorated** (760): honored

• **bicentennial** (760): 200th anniversary

• **mocked** (761): made fun of

■ CLASSIFYING INFORMATION Mark each statement *S* for elements of the Sunbelt's population increase or *F* for changing family life during the 1970s.

_____ **1.** An increasing number of Americans chose to live alone.

_____ **2.** Divorce was easier to get.

_____ **3.** The civil rights movement was a success.

_____ **4.** Citizens migrated from the North and East.

_____ **5.** Men and women waited longer to marry.

_____ **6.** Remarriage rates increased.

_____ **7.** The warmer climate attracted people.

_____ **8.** There were more job opportunities.

_____ **9.** Birthrates dropped.

_____ **10.** The number of single women raising children rose.

■ REVIEWING FACTS Choose the correct items from the following list to complete the statements below.

Steven Spielberg   Bilingual Education Act   smokers
rural   Neil Armstrong   disco
self-help books   motion pictures   fast food
Voting Rights Act of 1975

1. The _____ required states and communities with large numbers of non-English speakers to print voting materials in various foreign languages.

2. The _____ encouraged public schools to provide instruction to students in their primary languages while they learned English.

3. During the 1970s _____ became popular.

4. Many people moved to _____ areas to escape the tensions of modern life.

5. The number of _____ began to decline.

6. The popularity of _____ contributed to Americans' poor eating habits.

7. During the 1970s Americans spent more money than ever before on music and

_____.

8. _____ set a standard for great motion pictures.

9. Punk rock and _____ were popular forms of music in the 1970s.

10. _____ and Edwin Aldrin landed on the moon on July 20, 1969.

▨▨ **INTERPRETING VISUAL IMAGES** **Examine the picture below and answer the questions that follow.**

1. What is this a picture of?

_____

2. How did the work of Steven Jobs and Stephen Wozniak change people's everyday lives?

_____

_____

_____

The Republican Revolution

MAIN IDEA ACTIVITIES 26.1

■ VOCABULARY

An expression to understand:

• **industrial heartland (773):** geographic region in which industry is very strong

Other terms:

• **fundamentalist (771):** someone who believes in the Bible as a factual historic record
• **comprehensive (772):** large; well planned
• **stance (772):** position
• **instituted (774):** put into effect

■ ORGANIZING INFORMATION Complete the graphic organizer about the Iran hostage crisis by putting the following events in chronological order.

• In April 1980 a rescue mission failed when U.S. military helicopters crashed in the Iranian desert.
• Followers of Ayatollah Khomeini forced Mohammad Reza Pahlavi to leave Iran.
• Iranian militants took 53 American hostages at the U.S. embassy in Tehran.
• The hostages were freed on January 20, 1981.
• The United States helped overthrow Iran's leader and restore Shah Mohammad Reza Pahlavi to power.
• President Carter allowed Mohammad Reza Pahlavi into the United States for medical treatment.

Events of the Iran Hostage Crisis

1. _____
2. _____
3. _____
4. _____
5. _____
6. _____

■ CLASSIFYING INFORMATION Mark each of the following with either *A* (advantage) or *D* (disadvantage) of supply-side economics.

_____ **1.** The inflation rate dropped.

_____ **2.** Americans spent more money.

_____ **3.** Cuts in social programs hurt the poor.

_____ **4.** Businesses revived.

_____ **5.** Unemployment remained high among factory workers.

_____ **6.** The stock market soared.

_____ **7.** Homelessness increased.

■ EVALUATING INFORMATION Mark each statement *T* if it is true or *F* if it is false.

_____ **1.** During Reagan's campaign for the presidency he promised to "Make America strong again."

_____ **2.** The New Right was a group of political conservatives that included people with a strong background of fundamentalist Christian beliefs.

_____ **3.** Reagan and the New Right opposed school prayer, a strong defense, and free-market economic policies.

_____ **4.** Reagan and the New Right opposed abortion, the Equal Rights Amendment, gun control, and busing to achieve racial balance in schools.

_____ **5.** Reaganomics was President Reagan's economic program based on the theory of supply-side economics.

_____ **6.** During the Reagan administration the Cold War between the United States and the Soviet Union ended.

_____ **7.** President Reagan increased U.S. involvement in Latin America because he did not want it to fall under Soviet influence.

The Republican Revolution

MAIN IDEA ACTIVITIES 26.2

■ VOCABULARY

Some terms to understand:

• **federal deficit (778):** amount of money the United States owes others

• **across-the-board (778):** in every department

• **eroded (778):** wore away

• **funneled (779):** moved from various locations to a central site

• **defuse (782):** to make less harmful or tense

■ ORGANIZING INFORMATION Complete the chart by listing Mikhail Gorbachev's reform efforts for the Soviet Union.

Gorbachev's Reform of the Soviet Union
• _____
• _____
• _____
• _____
• _____
• _____

■ REVIEWING FACTS Choose the correct item from the following list to complete the statements below.

Gramm-Rudman-Hollings Act   women   Sandra Day O'Connor
insider trading   Grenada   Tax Reform Law of 1986
Oliver North   Geraldine Ferraro

1. In 1983 the United States sent military aid to _____ to overthrow leaders and set up a democratic government.

2. _____, Walter Mondale's running mate, was the first woman to run on a major-party presidential ticket.

3. President Reagan appointed several _____ to high public offices.

4. _____ was the first woman to serve on the Supreme Court.

5. The _____ required automatic across-the-board cuts in government spending whenever the deficit exceeded a certain amount.

6. The _____ eliminated special tax breaks that certain groups had been receiving.

7. The use of confidential financial information for personal gain within the stock market is

called _____.

8. _____ funneled millions of dollars from Iranian arms sales to the Contras in Nicaragua.

The Republican Revolution

CHAPTER 26

MAIN IDEA ACTIVITIES 26.3

■ VOCABULARY

Some terms to understand:

• **vast array (783):** a lot to choose from   • **spawned (784):** gave birth to

■ EVALUATING INFORMATION Mark each statement *T* if it is true or *F* if it is false.

_____ **1.** Most families benefited from the economic boom of the 1980s.

_____ **2.** Single-parent families were not common during the 1980s.

_____ **3.** The 1980s brought a vast array of new electronic goods.

_____ **4.** The space program had declined during the 1970s due to rising costs and a lack of interest.

_____ **5.** After the *Challenger* exploded, shuttle flights were suspended for two months.

_____ **6.** President Bush did not think that the United States needed to be a world leader; he thought it should just take care of its own problems.

_____ **7.** The Persian Gulf War was won almost entirely by using high-tech weapons.

_____ **8.** President Bush was an extremely strong supporter of education.

_____ **9.** Congress passed almost all of Bush's legislation for education.

_____ **10.** Because he was charged with sexual harassment, Clarence Thomas lost the nomination to the Supreme Court.

■ REVIEWING FACTS Choose the correct items from the following list to complete the statements below.

Commonwealth of Independent States	Boris Yeltsin
Jesse Jackson	AIDS
Christa McAuliffe	Soviet Union
Operation Desert Storm	William Gibson
women	Republican

1. _____ published the science fiction book *Neuromancer* that warned of a future in which technology takes over the world.

2. _____ was a teacher who died when the space shuttle *Challenger* exploded.

3. Doctors reported the first case of _____ in 1981; it killed hundreds of thousands of people by the end of the decade.

4. In 1984 _____ helped generate the largest turnout ever of African American voters in a primary election.

5. The 1988 _____ presidential campaign was controversial because it focused on negative issues.

6. In 1989 the _____ announced that it was adopting a policy of nonintervention in Eastern Europe.

7. When Gorbachev resigned as president of the Soviet Union, he turned control of the armed

forces over to _____.

8. The _____ was a loose confederation of Belarus, Russia, Ukraine, and other former Soviet republics.

9. _____ was the allied response to Iraq's refusal to withdraw from Kuwait.

10. In August 1991 the Senate removed the ban on _____ serving as combat pilots, but continued to limit female soldiers' roles in ground battles.

■■ **ORGANIZING INFORMATION** **Complete the graphic organizer about the U.S. space program using the following items.**

• send a civilian on a shuttle trip
• rising costs
• failing interest in missions
• make a reusable space shuttle

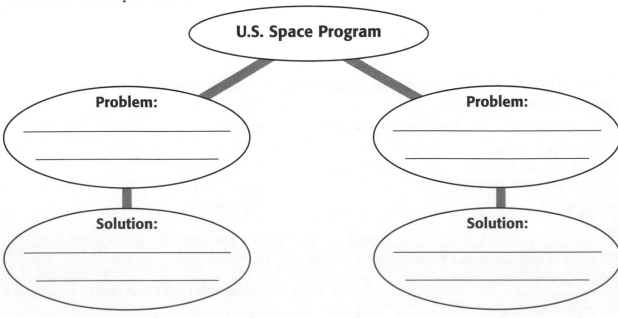

Launching the New Millennium

MAIN IDEA ACTIVITIES 27.1

◼ VOCABULARY

A term to understand:

• **dub** (799): nickname

◼ ORGANIZING INFORMATION Complete the chart about the 1992 presidential election candidates using the following items.

• promised to decrease the influence of political lobbyists

• focused on the personal character of the candidates

• promised to give the public a greater voice in government

• promised governmental renewal

• promised to use his business skills to balance the budget

Ross Perot	Bill Clinton	George Bush
• _____	• _____	• _____
_____	_____	_____
• _____		
_____		
• _____		
_____		

◼ CLASSIFYING INFORMATION Identify each event with *E* (Eastern Europe), *S* (former Soviet Union), or *A* (South Africa) to show where it occurred during the 1990s.

_____ **1.** Decades of white-only rule came to an end, and Nelson Mandela was elected president.

_____ **2.** Christians in Armenia battled with Muslims in Azerbaijan.

_____ **3.** The end of communist rule unleashed bitter ethnic and local disputes that had formerly been kept in check by communist authorities.

_____ **4.** Russia and Ukraine argued over control of the Black Sea fleet.

▨▨ UNDERSTANDING MAIN IDEAS For each of the following, write the letter of the *best* choice in the space provided.

_____ 1. Which of these statements does *NOT* describe Hillary Rodham Clinton?
   a. was a lawyer
   b. served as a staff member with the House Judiciary Committee
   c. became vice president
   d. headed a task force to reform the nation's health care system

_____ 2. Why was 1992 called "the year of the woman"?
   a. There was a large increase in the number of female candidates.
   b. More women were working outside of the home.
   c. Women received the right to vote.
   d. There were more females born than males.

_____ 3. Which of these did *NOT* happen due to the 1993 budget act that combined tax increases and spending cuts?
   a. Unemployment dropped.
   b. The deficit dropped.
   c. Inflation increased.
   d. The stock market boomed.

_____ 4. In December 1992 UN forces launched Operation Restore Hope to provide relief to famine-stricken
   a. Armenia.
   b. Bosnia.
   c. Azerbaijan.
   d. Somalia.

_____ 5. With the end of the Cold War, _____ increased throughout the world.
   a. starvation
   b. Christianity
   c. terrorist activity
   d. communism

_____ 6. President Clinton ordered the bombing of Iraqi intelligence service headquarters after the FBI uncovered an Iraqi plot to assassinate former president
   a. Jimmy Carter.
   b. George Bush.
   c. Gerald Ford.
   d. Richard Nixon.

CHAPTER
27

Launching the New Millennium

MAIN IDEA ACTIVITIES 27.2

▓ VOCABULARY

A term to understand:

• **boom (805):** period of growth

▓ ORGANIZING INFORMATION Complete the chart about U.S. race relations during the Clinton administration, using the following items.

• white racists in Jasper, Texas, killed James Byrd Jr.

• called for tougher federal laws against hate crimes

• launched the Initiative on Race to encourage people to discuss racial issues and concerns

• violence exploded in Los Angeles after four white police officers were acquitted of beating Rodney King

U.S. Race Relations

Event	Response
• _____ _____	• _____ _____
• _____ _____	• _____ _____

▓ EVALUATING INFORMATION Mark each statement *T* if it is true or *F* if it is false.

_____ **1.** Bob Dole tried to present himself as a mature and dignified candidate.

_____ **2.** Bob Dole's age was a concern during the 1996 campaign.

_____ **3.** Bob Dole was an extremely effective speaker and campaigner.

_____ **4.** Bill Clinton was the first Democratic president since Franklin D. Roosevelt to win a second term.

_____ **5.** After the 1996 election Democrats maintained a majority in both the House and Senate.

_____ **6.** During the 1990s the United States experienced the longest and largest economic boom in history.

■■ **UNDERSTANDING MAIN IDEAS** **For each of the following, write the letter of the *best* choice in the space provided.**

_____ **1.** Much of the new wealth of the 1990s was the result of
   a. more people working.
   b. rising oil prices.
   c. the booming stock market.
   d. lower interest rates.

_____ **2.** Which of these did *NOT* happen during the 1990s?
   a. Unemployment stayed low.
   b. Inflation rates stayed low.
   c. Interest rates stayed low.
   d. American morale stayed low.

_____ **3.** The House Judiciary Committee recommended impeachment of President Clinton because
   a. he cheated on his taxes.
   b. he lied under oath and tried to obstruct justice.
   c. his morals were questionable.
   d. he was involved in questionable financial investments.

_____ **4.** Who was the first female secretary of state for the United States?
   a. Madeleine Albright
   b. Hillary Rodham Clinton
   c. Janet Reno
   d. Eleanor Smeal

_____ **5.** President Slobodan Milosevic of Yugoslavia withdrew his troops from Kosovo due to
   a. Kosovo's strong military.
   b. an illness that left him unable to command his forces.
   c. peace talks with Jimmy Carter.
   d. NATO's air strikes against Kosovo.

CHAPTER 27 Launching the New Millennium

MAIN IDEA ACTIVITIES 27.3

■ VOCABULARY

An expression to understand:

• **mass culture (812):** because the United States is so large and affects so many other cultures, it is called a mass culture

Other terms:

• **breathtaking (810):** very beautiful or exciting
• **consecutive (810):** following one after the other in order
• **orbit (810):** travel around
• **indecency (811):** being offensive or not in good taste

■ ORGANIZING INFORMATION Complete the chart about recent immigration to the United States, using the following items.

• Immigrants take jobs from native-born residents.
• Immigrants create new businesses that help the economy.
• Immigrants have, on the average, more education than native-born Americans.
• Large numbers of immigrants who are willing to work for lower wages decrease wages for all workers.

Recent Immigration

Supporters	Opponents
• _____ _____	• _____ _____
• _____ _____	• _____ _____

▨ REVIEWING FACTS Choose the correct item from the following list to complete the statements below.

Family and Medical Leave Act	Hubble Space Telescope
Shannon Lucid	Telecommunications Act
Internet	Bill Gates
World Wide Web	John Glenn

1. The _____ was launched in 1990. It transmitted information and photos from deep space.

2. _____ spent 188 days in space aboard the space station *Mir*.

3. _____ was the first person to orbit Earth, and this individual also became the oldest American to fly in space.

4. _____ was a leader in the computer revolution.

5. The _____ is a computer-based communications and information system that enables users to communicate worldwide and gather information from databases.

6. The _____ links Internet sites.

7. Key parts of the _____ were struck down by a federal court as a violation of free-speech rights.

8. The _____ requires large companies to provide workers up to 12 weeks of unpaid leave for family and medical emergencies without losing their medical coverage or their jobs.

Main Idea Activities

Launching the New Millennium

MAIN IDEA ACTIVITIES 27.4

■ VOCABULARY

A term to understand:

• **bloc** (815): group of people or nations united for a common action

■ ORGANIZING INFORMATION Complete the chart about national issues, using the following items.

• The California Desert Protection Act converted two national monuments to national parks.
• People called for increased funding for research on alternative energy sources.
• Greenpeace campaigned against whaling.
• Recycling programs emerged.

National Issues

Concerns	Actions
Nuclear Power	• _____ _____
Wildlife	• _____ _____ • _____ _____
Natural Resources	• _____ _____

■ EVALUATING INFORMATION Mark each statement *T* if it is true or *F* if it is false.

_____ 1. International trading blocs may provide stiff economic competition for the United States in coming years.

_____ 2. The European Union was designed to allow for the free movement of capital, goods, and labor among member nations.

_____ 3. Some experts predict that at least 20 European nations will eventually form a political union.

_____ 4. The North American Free Trade Agreement made trade more difficult among the United States, Mexico, and Canada.

_____ 5. Multinational corporations are a negative influence on our economy.

_____ 6. In 1996 the United States accounted for nearly 25 percent of the world's energy consumption.

_____ 7. The accident at the Chernobyl nuclear power plant produced more radioactive material than the two bombs dropped on Hiroshima and Nagasaki combined.

_____ 8. President Clinton used the Antiquities Act to create the Canyons of the Escalante National Monument without congressional approval.

_____ 9. The United States leads the world in recycling.

_____ 10. Many of the world's environmental and waste problems have been made worse by a large increase in population.

_____ 11. Democratic presidential candidate Al Gore won the 2000 election by a wide margin.

_____ 12. The 2000 presidential election led to calls for reform in the electoral college system.

Answer Key

CHAPTER 1

MAIN IDEA ACTIVITIES 1.1

ORGANIZING INFORMATION

Maya—Southern Mexico and Guatemala—devised a number system and wrote with glyphs

Aztec—Central Mexico—developed a canal system

Inca—Andes of South America—was the largest empire in the Americas

EVALUATING INFORMATION

1. F
2. F
3. T
4. T
5. T
6. F
7. T
8. F
9. T
10. T

REVIEWING FACTS

1. Paleo-Indians
2. Agricultural Revolution
3. China
4. Ghana
5. feudalism
6. Crusades
7. monarchies
8. *encomienda*
9. Hernán Cortés
10. Francisco Pizarro

MAIN IDEA ACTIVITIES 1.2

CLASSIFYING INFORMATION

1. b
2. b
3. a
4. c
5. b
6. b
7. c
8. a
9. a
10. c
11. b
12. c
13. a

EVALUATING INFORMATION

1. F
2. T
3. F
4. F
5. T
6. T
7. T
8. F

UNDERSTANDING MAIN IDEAS

1. b
2. d
3. a
4. b

MAIN IDEA ACTIVITIES 1.3

CLASSIFYING INFORMATION

1. Treaty of Paris of 1763
2. Proclamation of 1763
3. Stamp Act
4. Declaratory Act
5. Tea Act
6. Coercive Acts
7. Olive Branch Petition
8. Declaration of Independence
9. Treaty of Paris of 1783

EVALUATING INFORMATION

1. F
2. T
3. T
4. F
5. T
6. T
7. T
8. F

REVIEWING FACTS

1. Samuel Adams
2. Boston Massacre
3. Boston Tea Party

4. Paul Revere

5. Thomas Jefferson

6. Trenton

7. Saratoga

8. Paris

MAIN IDEA ACTIVITIES 1.4

ORGANIZING INFORMATION

Articles—Shays's Rebellion revealed its weaknesses; proposed changes required the consent of all 13 states; went into effect in 1781; one-house legislature

Constitution—created a government based on federalism; two-house legislature; went into effect in 1788; created three branches of government

EVALUATING INFORMATION

1. T

2. T

3. F

4. T

5. T

6. F

7. F

8. T

UNDERSTANDING MAIN IDEAS

1. b

2. d

3. a

4. d

5. b

6. c

CHAPTER 2

MAIN IDEA ACTIVITIES 2.1

ORGANIZING INFORMATION

Democratic-Republicans; John Adams and Alexander Hamilton; states' rights, limited government power, supported France

EVALUATING INFORMATION

1. T

2. T

3. F

4. F

5. F

6. T

7. T

8. F

9. F

10. T

11. F

12. T

13. T

14. T

15. T

16. T

17. F

MAIN IDEA ACTIVITIES 2.2

EVALUATING INFORMATION

1. F

2. T

3. T

4. F

5. T

6. F

7. F

8. F

REVIEWING FACTS

1. Monroe Doctrine

2. American System

3. Missouri Compromise

4. Indian Removal Act

5. strike

6. nativism

7. Underground Railroad

8. Second Great Awakening

9. American Anti-Slavery Society

10. Seneca Falls Convention

UNDERSTANDING MAIN IDEAS

1. b

2. c

3. b

4. a

MAIN IDEA ACTIVITIES 2.3

ORGANIZING INFORMATION

Texas Revolution

Cause—The Mexican government closed the Mexican border to Americans and President Santa Anna declared himself dictator.

Outcome—Texas was granted independence in 1836.

Mexican War

Cause— A Mexican attack on U.S. troops along the disputed Texas-Mexico border.

Outcome—Mexico gave up all claims to Texas and surrendered the Mexican Cession.

EVALUATING INFORMATION

1. T
2. F
3. T
4. T
5. F
6. T
7. F
8. T

REVIEWING FACTS

1. manifest destiny
2. popular sovereignty
3. Harriet Beecher Stowe
4. John Brown
5. *Dred Scott* decision
6. Confederate States of America

CHAPTER 3

MAIN IDEA ACTIVITIES 3.1

ORGANIZING INFORMATION

Delaware: Because it had few slaves, its people sympathized with the North.

Kentucky: Citizens were divided over the issue; the governor sympathized with the North so the state did not secede.

Maryland: It was secured by federal troops in an effort to bar secession.

Missouri: Citizens were divided over the issue; the governor sympathized with the North so the state did not secede.

Northwestern Virginia: It remained loyal to the Union.

Upper South: Citizens fought on both sides of the war.

CLASSIFYING INFORMATION

1. N
2. S
3. N
4. S
5. N
6. N

EVALUATING INFORMATION

1. T
2. T
3. F
4. T
5. F
6. T
7. T
8. F
9. T
10. T
11. F
12. F
13. F
14. T
15. T

MAIN IDEA ACTIVITIES 3.2

CLASSIFYING INFORMATION

1. N
2. S
3. N
4. N
5. N
6. S

ORGANIZING INFORMATION

North

Women worked as clerks in the Treasury Department.

Female schoolteachers educated former slaves.

Both

Women replaced male workers who were fighting in the war.

South

Women held patriotic events to urge young men to join the army.

Women held raffles to raise funds for the army.

REVIEWING FACTS

1. Anaconda Plan
2. Mississippi River
3. shortages
4. blue
5. gray

6. Confederate
7. illness
8. Andersonville, Georgia
9. Loreta Janeta Velázquez
10. spies
11. Catholic nuns
12. Clara Barton
13. Sally Louisa Tompkins
14. farmers
15. Union Draft Law
16. Copperheads

MAIN IDEA ACTIVITIES 3.3

EVALUATING INFORMATION

1. F
2. T
3. F
4. T
5. T
6. F
7. F
8. T

REVIEWING FACTS

1. Battle of Shiloh
2. Seven Days' Battle
3. Emancipation Proclamation
4. Battle of Antietam
5. 54th Massachusetts Infantry
6. African American

UNDERSTANDING MAIN IDEAS

1. b
2. d
3. a
4. d
5. c

MAIN IDEA ACTIVITIES 3.4

ORGANIZING INFORMATION

July 1: The Confederates pushed the Union line back to Cemetery Hill and Cemetery Ridge.

July 2: General Lee charged the Union's left flank, but did not capture Little Round Top.

July 3: General Lee ordered 15,000 men to rush the Union center on Cemetery Ridge.

REVIEWING FACTS

1. Chancellorsville
2. Gettysburg Address
3. Siege of Vicksburg
4. war of attrition
5. William T. Sherman
6. Appalachian Mountains
7. total war

UNDERSTANDING MAIN IDEAS

1. d
2. c
3. d
4. b

CHAPTER 4

MAIN IDEA ACTIVITIES 4.1

ORGANIZING INFORMATION

He removed African American troops.
He recognized Mississippi's new government.

EVALUATING INFORMATION

1. F
2. F
3. T
4. F
5. T
6. T
7. T

REVIEWING FACTS

1. Thirteenth Amendment
2. Proclamation of Amnesty and Reconstruction
3. Wade-Davis Bill
4. President Andrew Johnson
5. John Wilkes Booth
6. Sidney George Fisher
7. Black Codes
8. Alexander H. Stevens
9. African Americans

MAIN IDEA ACTIVITIES 4.2

ORGANIZING INFORMATION

1. moderate and Radical Republicans join forces
2. Congress passes Freedmen's Bureau Bill
3. Johnson vetoes Freedmen's Bureau Bill

4. Congress passes Civil Rights Act of 1866
5. Johnson vetoes Civil Rights Act of 1866
6. Fourteenth Amendment passes
7. elections of 1866 give Republicans control of Congress
8. Congress passes Reconstruction Acts of 1867
9. Congress passes Tenure of Office Act
10. Johnson removes Secretary of War Edwin Stanton

EVALUATING INFORMATION

1. F
2. T
3. T
4. T
5. F
6. T
7. T
8. T
9. F

MAIN IDEA ACTIVITIES 4.3

ORGANIZING INFORMATION

Panic of 1873: Voters turned against the Republican-controlled Congress; Republican Party's interest in universal voting rights faded; Republicans abandoned universal voting rights.

Compromise of 1877: Republicans agreed to withdraw remaining federal troops from the South; Democrats in some southern states used terrorism to prevent African Americans from voting for the Republican Party.

REVIEWING FACTS

1. Union
2. read
3. vote
4. Nathan Bedford Forrest
5. military
6. immigrants
7. Panic of 1873
8. government
9. discriminating
10. Compromise of 1877

MAIN IDEA ACTIVITIES 4.4

ORGANIZING INFORMATION

advantages
farmers had a place to live
planters did not have to pay in cash
workers got a portion of profit from crops

disadvantages
led to the crop-lien system
encouraged growing only one crop
easy to build debt

REVIEWING FACTS

1. cotton
2. Henry W. Grady
3. Jim Crow laws
4. Homer Plessy
5. Justice John Marshall Harlan
6. cooperatives
7. Madame C. J. Walker
8. Booker T. Washington
9. Ida B. Wells

CHAPTER 5

MAIN IDEA ACTIVITIES 5.1

ORGANIZING INFORMATION

1. **Agency:** Bureau of Indian Affairs
2. **Actions Affecting American Indians**
   reduced size of reservations
   forced them to farm
   forced them to abandon their traditions
   forced them to move
3. **Benefit for White Settlers**
   opened land for settlement

EVALUATING INFORMATION

1. T
2. T
3. F
4. F
5. T
6. F
7. T
8. T

UNDERSTANDING MAIN IDEAS

1. c
2. b

3. c
4. a
5. b
6. d

MAIN IDEA ACTIVITIES 5.2

ORGANIZING INFORMATION

1. From—the East; Reasons for Move—in search of more fertile soil, to make a new start, so their children could grow up with the country
2. Group—African Americans; Reasons for Move—to escape violence and persecution
3. From—Denmark (Danes), Norway (Norwegians), Sweden (Swedes), Ireland (Irish), Germany (Germans), Russia (Russians); Reason for Move—"American Fever"

UNDERSTANDING MAIN IDEAS

1. a
2. b
3. b
4. c
5. d
6. d

MAIN IDEA ACTIVITIES 5.3

EVALUATING INFORMATION

1. T
2. T
3. F
4. T
5. T
6. T

UNDERSTANDING MAIN IDEAS

1. b
2. c
3. a
4. c
5. d
6. a
7. c
8. b

MAIN IDEA ACTIVITIES 5.4

CLASSIFYING INFORMATION

1. A
2. B
3. B
4. A
5. A
6. A

REVIEWING FACTS

1. Hispanic
2. Klondike Gold Rush
3. Cripple Creek
4. arguments over claims
5. mining camps
6. Hydraulic mining
7. breathe
8. William Kelley
9. union

INTERPRETING VISUAL IMAGES

1. a sluice
2. searching for precious metals or gold and silver
3. in Alaska or the West

CHAPTER 6

MAIN IDEA ACTIVITIES 6.1

ORGANIZING INFORMATION

Answers **1** and **2** and answers **3** and **4** can be in either order.

1. **Bessemer process**—produced more steel in a day than previously produced in a week
2. **Holley's adaptation**—American steel production increased dramatically
3. **process to refine oil**—could be turned into kerosene
4. **Drake's Folly**—flow of oil from well at vastly increased rate

UNDERSTANDING MAIN IDEAS

1. c
2. a
3. d
4. b
5. c
6. d
7. a

Main Idea Activities

8. c
9. c
10. d

MAIN IDEA ACTIVITIES 6.2

ORGANIZING INFORMATION
1. Andrew Carnegie
2. John D. Rockefeller
3. Cornelius Vanderbilt

EVALUATING INFORMATION
1. F
2. T
3. T
4. F
5. F
6. T
7. T

REVIEWING FACTS
1. Gospel of Wealth
2. Andrew Carnegie
3. vertical integration
4. John D. Rockefeller
5. railroad
6. marketing
7. Sears, Roebuck, and Co.
8. department stores
9. large quantities

MAIN IDEA ACTIVITIES 6.3

ORGANIZING INFORMATION
Second Industrial Age
ten- to twelve-hour work days
six- to seven-day workweeks
minorities paid less for the same job
no compensation for injury on the job

Today
company-paid health insurance
paid vacations
retirement plans
safe working environment

UNDERSTANDING MAIN IDEAS
1. c
2. a
3. c
4. b
5. d

6. a
7. b
8. a
9. c
10. a

CHAPTER 7

MAIN IDEA ACTIVITIES 7.1

ORGANIZING INFORMATION
old immigrants
from northwestern Europe
Protestant

new immigrants
arrived in America from 1891 to 1910
Catholic, Greek Orthodox, or Jewish

in common
wanted to escape poverty
willing to endure many hardships

EVALUATING INFORMATION
1. T
2. F
3. T
4. T
5. F
6. T

REVIEWING FACTS
1. Statue of Liberty
2. steamship lines
3. Angel Island
4. benevolent societies
5. jobs
6. Workingmen's Party of California
7. citizens
8. literacy tests
9. industry

MAIN IDEA ACTIVITIES 7.2

EVALUATING INFORMATION
1. F
2. T
3. T
4. F
5. T
6. F

UNDERSTANDING MAIN IDEAS

1. a
2. c
3. d
4. c
5. b
6. a
7. d
8. c
9. b
10. c

MAIN IDEA ACTIVITIES 7.3

EVALUATING INFORMATION

1. T
2. F
3. T
4. T
5. T
6. F
7. F
8. T

REVIEWING FACTS

1. John Dewey
2. Edith Wharton
3. bicycling
4. Cincinnati Red Stockings
5. football
6. spectator sports
7. Edwin Booth
8. vaudeville
9. dances

ORGANIZING INFORMATION

Baseball
evolved from a British game
had professional leagues
excluded African American players

Football
evolved from a British game
had professional leagues
many serious injuries during early years of
    play

Basketball
invented in the United States
women encouraged to play

CHAPTER 8

MAIN IDEA ACTIVITIES 8.1

ORGANIZING INFORMATION

Advantages
provided jobs to local residents
could provide political favors and services

Disadvantages
encouraged graft and corruption
interfered with important functions of city
    governments

REVIEWING FACTS

1. political machines
2. immigrants
3. Irish Americans
4. voting fraud
5. public
6. Charles Tyson Yerkes
7. James Pendergast
8. Tammany Hall
9. cartoons

MAIN IDEA ACTIVITIES 8.2

ORGANIZING INFORMATION

1. Liberal Republican Party was formed
2. Whiskey Ring scandal
3. Stalwarts and Half-Breeds split Republicans
4. President Garfield assassinated
5. Pendleton Civil Service Act passed
6. Republican Congress weakened civil service reform movement

REVIEWING FACTS

1. gold
2. Liberal Republican Party
3. Mark Twain
4. Stalwarts
5. merit
6. Chester A. Arthur
7. Pendleton Civil Service Act
8. an honest man
9. Benjamin Harrison

MAIN IDEA ACTIVITIES 8.3

CLASSIFYING INFORMATION

National Grange
active with railroad freight rates
first major farmers' organization

Main Idea Activities

Farmers' Alliance
worked for graduated income tax
fought for tougher bank regulations

Both
formed cooperatives to help members
supported the Populist Party
wanted the silver standard

UNDERSTANDING MAIN IDEAS
1. b
2. c
3. d
4. a
5. b
6. d
7. a
8. c
9. a
10. c

CHAPTER 9

MAIN IDEA ACTIVITIES 9.1

ORGANIZING INFORMATION
big business
end child labor
minimum wage

social justice
public education
journalism that exposed harmful social issues

democracy
election reforms
greater control in all areas of government

REVIEWING FACTS
1. progressivism
2. middle class
3. women
4. social reform
5. Social Gospel
6. John D. Rockefeller
7. lynching
8. muckrakers
9. Herbert Croly

MAIN IDEA ACTIVITIES 9.2

ORGANIZING INFORMATION
AFL
skilled workers only
major labor organization of the time

ILGWU
mainly Jewish and Italian immigrant women
received strike support from Women's Trade
    Union League

IWW
members from minority races
against capitalism

EVALUATING INFORMATION
1. T
2. T
3. F
4. T

REVIEWING FACTS
1. Commission on Industrial Relations
2. National Child Labor Committee
3. fire-safety
4. Brandeis Brief
5. Fourteenth Amendment
6. closed shop
7. socialism
8. International Ladies' Garment Workers
    Union
8. Industrial Workers of the World

MAIN IDEA ACTIVITIES 9.3

EVALUATING INFORMATION
1. F
2. T
3. F
4. T
5. T
6. T

UNDERSTANDING MAIN IDEAS
1. d
2. b
3. a
4. c
5. a
6. c

Changes: buildings built around courtyards; let in light and air

CHAPTER 10

MAIN IDEA ACTIVITIES 10.1

CLASSIFYING INFORMATION
initiative
referendum
recall

REVIEWING FACTS
1. U.S. Senate
2. election process
3. direct primary
4. secret ballot
5. Samuel M. "Golden Rule" Jones
6. voter
7. lower classes
8. city commission
9. city manager
10. Wisconsin Idea
11. African Americans
12. Robert M. La Follette

MAIN IDEA ACTIVITIES 10.2

EVALUATING INFORMATION
1. F
2. F
3. T
4. F
5. T
6. T

UNDERSTANDING MAIN IDEAS
1. c
2. a
3. b
4. a
5. c
6. d
7. b
8. d
9. a
10. d

MAIN IDEA ACTIVITIES 10.3

ORGANIZING INFORMATION
Taft
presidential power limited by Constitution
supported Richard Ballinger
did not oppose high tariffs

Progressive Party
expand presidential power
supported Gifford Pinchot
wanted low tariffs

REVIEWING FACTS
1. Mann-Elkins Act
2. Payne-Aldrich Tariff
3. conservation
4. New Nationalism
5. Joseph "Uncle Joe" Cannon
6. Theodore Roosevelt
7. Bull Moose Party
8. Woodrow Wilson
9. New Freedom

MAIN IDEA ACTIVITIES 10.4

ORGANIZING INFORMATION
bank—Federal Reserve Act
injured man—Federal Workmen's Compensation Act
woman with ballot—Nineteenth Amendment
farm tractor—Federal Farm Loan Act
factory—Clayton Antitrust Act

REVIEWING FACTS
1. graduated income tax
2. Federal Trade Commission
3. child labor
4. National American Woman Suffrage Association
5. National Woman's Party
6. Carrie Chapman Catt
7. African Americans

CHAPTER 11

MAIN IDEA ACTIVITIES 11.1

ORGANIZING INFORMATION
Henry Cabot Lodge—dollar bills and soldiers
Alfred Thayer Mahan—steamship at dock
Josiah Strong—books and cross

EVALUATING INFORMATION

1. T
2. T
3. F
4. F
5. T
6. T
7. T
8. T
9. F
10. T

MAIN IDEA ACTIVITIES 11.2

EVALUATING INFORMATION

1. T
2. T
3. F
4. T
5. F
6. F

UNDERSTANDING MAIN IDEAS

1. b
2. c
3. a
4. b
5. a
6. d
7. c
8. d

MAIN IDEA ACTIVITIES 11.3

ORGANIZING INFORMATION

Theodore Roosevelt
Roosevelt Corollary
Dominican Republic

William H. Taft
dollar diplomacy
Nicaragua

Woodrow Wilson
democratic government
Haiti

REVIEWING FACTS

1. Cuba
2. Puerto Rico
3. John Hay
4. Philippe Bunau-Varilla
5. Panama

6. yellow fever
7. Path Between the Seas
8. Theodore Roosevelt
9. Hemisphere

MAIN IDEA ACTIVITIES 11.4

ORGANIZING INFORMATION

1. Porfirio Díaz takes power
2. Zapata rebels
3. Francisco Madero wins elections
4. Victoriano Huerta seizes control
5. U.S. troops in Veracruz
6. Pancho Villa attacks Columbus, New Mexico
7. General Pershing arrives in Mexico
8. U.S. troops withdrawn
9. Venustiano Carranza takes power
10. new Mexican constitution created

EVALUATING INFORMATION

1. T
2. T
3. F
4. F
5. T
6. T
7. F
8. T
9. F
10. T
11. F
12. T

CHAPTER 12

MAIN IDEA ACTIVITIES 12.1

EVALUATING INFORMATION

1. T
2. F
3. T
4. T
5. T
6. T

REVIEWING FACTS

1. powder keg
2. militarism
3. Archduke Franz Ferdinand

4. Allied Powers
5. Central Powers
6. Schlieffen Plan
7. trench warfare
8. Battle of the Somme

INTERPRETING VISUAL IMAGES
1. Any two of the following: plane, tank, poison gas
2. barbed wire
3. poison gas

MAIN IDEA ACTIVITIES 12.2

ORGANIZING INFORMATION
Wilson's Policy
Be neutral: in fact as well as in name

Britain's Actions
Blockaded: Germany
Laid mines: in the North Sea
Stopped U.S. ships: and searched cargoes

Germany's Actions
Established a war zone: around Britain
Said ships entering it: were subject to attack
March 28, 1915: sank a British passenger liner
May 7, 1915: sank the *Lusitania*

American Reaction
Congress in June 1916: passed the National Defense Act

UNDERSTANDING MAIN IDEAS
1. b
2. a
3. c
4. a
5. b
6. c
7. b
8. c
9. a
10. d

MAIN IDEA ACTIVITIES 12.3

CLASSIFYING INFORMATION
Food Administration
Herbert Hoover
farm production increased

Fuel Administration
William McAdoo
temporarily closed coal plants

Railroad Administration
Harry Garfield
limited transportation rates

REVIEWING FACTS
1. Liberty bonds
2. War Industries
3. labor
4. women
5. Nineteenth Amendment
6. volunteerism
7. Juliette Gordon Low
8. Great Migration
9. Committee on Public Information
10. Bernard Baruch
11. liberty pups
12. Espionage and Sedition Acts

MAIN IDEA ACTIVITIES 12.4

CLASSIFYING INFORMATION
Belgium must be evacuated and restored—territorial dispute
People of Austria-Hungary should be accorded the freest opportunity of autonomous development—self-determination
Readjust the frontiers of Italy along clearly recognizable lines of nationality—territorial dispute
Romania, Serbia, and Montenegro should be evacuated—territorial dispute

EVALUATING INFORMATION
1. T
2. T
3. F
4. T
5. F
6. T
7. T
8. T
9. T

CHAPTER 13

MAIN IDEA ACTIVITIES 13.1

CLASSIFYING INFORMATION
1. Seattle general strike
2. Boston police strike
3. Steel strike
4. United Mine Workers strike

UNDERSTANDING MAIN IDEAS
1. d
2. a
3. b
4. a
5. b
6. d
7. b
8. a
9. d
10. b

MAIN IDEA ACTIVITIES 13.2

ORGANIZING INFORMATION
Positives
business profits increased
surplus from tax cuts helped the economy

Negatives
farmers driven deeply into debt
loss of some Progressive Era labor reforms

REVIEWING FACTS
1. farmers
2. Andrew Mellon
3. yellow-dog contracts
4. League of Women Voters
5. women
6. oil reserves
7. Revenue Act of 1926
8. Calvin Coolidge
9. Alfred E. Smith

MAIN IDEA ACTIVITIES 13.3

ORGANIZING INFORMATION
Bursum Bill
picture b
Southwest Pueblo Indians

Marcus Garve
picture c
Universal Negro Improvement Association

A. Philip Randolph
picture a
Brotherhood of Sleeping Car Porters

EVALUATING INFORMATION
1. T
2. T
3. T
4. F
5. T
6. F
7. T
8. T
9. F
10. T
11. T

CHAPTER 14

MAIN IDEA ACTIVITIES 14.1

EVALUATING INFORMATION
1. T
2. F
3. T
4. T
5. F
6. F

UNDERSTANDING MAIN IDEAS
1. b
2. c
3. d
4. a
5. c
6. d
7. b
8. a
9. d
10. a

MAIN IDEA ACTIVITIES 14.2

EVALUATING INFORMATION
1. T
2. T

3. F
4. T
5. F
6. T

REVIEWING FACTS

1. commercial
2. radio
3. *The Jazz Singer*
4. professional sports
5. Book-of-the-Month Club
6. Babe Ruth
7. Charles Lindbergh
8. revivalist
9. Fundamentalism
10. Scopes trial

INTERPRETING VISUAL IMAGES

bobbed hair
short skirts
transparent hose

MAIN IDEA ACTIVITIES 14.3

CLASSIFYING INFORMATION

Musicians
Louis Armstrong
Bessie Smith

Writers
Langston Hughes
Claude McKay

Actors
Paul Robeson
Rose McClendon

REVIEWING FACTS

1. jazz
2. George Gershwin
3. Cotton Club
4. equal rights
5. Lost Generation
6. middle-class
7. Alfred Stieglitz
8. Diego Rivera
9. Mexican Renaissance
10. skyscrapers
11. Frank Lloyd Wright
12. Empire State

CHAPTER 15

MAIN IDEA ACTIVITIES 15.1

ORGANIZING INFORMATION

1. Stock market crashes.
2. Borrowers cannot repay bank loans.
3. Some banks fail.
4. Panicky customers withdraw money.
5. More banks fail.

UNDERSTANDING MAIN IDEAS

1. c
2. d
3. a
4. b
5. d
6. b
7. a
8. a
9. b

MAIN IDEA ACTIVITIES 15.2

ORGANIZING INFORMATION

At home people
read books
played board games
listened to the radio

More people went to the movies because
double features
low ticket prices

What people saw
any four of the following: gangster films, films about strong women, Bette Davis, Greta Garbo, Mae West, Marlene Dietrich, cartoons, Mickey Mouse, Donald Duck

REVIEWING FACTS

1. immigration
2. African Americans
3. Bronx Slave Market
4. skilled craftsmen
5. cities
6. Hoovervilles
7. farmers
8. Mexicans
9. roles
10. birthrate
11. hope
12. financial stability

MAIN IDEA ACTIVITIES 15.3

ORGANIZING INFORMATION

Reconstruction Finance Corporation—stabilize troubled financial institutions

Federal Farm Board—purchase surplus farm products

Home Loan Bank Act—reduce foreclosures on homes and farms

President's Committee for Unemployment Relief—encourage donations to private relief organizations

EVALUATING INFORMATION
1. F
2. T
3. F
4. T

REVIEWING FACTS
1. Salvation Army
2. Federal Emergency Relief Board
3. capitalism
4. army
5. Franklin Delano Roosevelt
6. depression
7. Congress

CHAPTER 16

MAIN IDEA ACTIVITIES 16.1

EVALUATING INFORMATION
1. F
2. T
3. T
4. F
5. T

REVIEWING FACTS
1. Federal Deposit Insurance Corporation
2. Farm Credit Administration
3. Home Owners Loan Corporation
4. Federal Emergency Relief Administration
5. Civil Works Administration
6. Agricultural Adjustment Administration

UNDERSTANDING MAIN IDEAS
1. b
2. d
3. c
4. a
5. d
6. a
7. a

MAIN IDEA ACTIVITIES 16.2

ORGANIZING INFORMATION
1. Farm Credit Administration; To refinance farm mortgages
2. CCC; To employ young men
3. TVA; Tennessee Valley Authority
4. Home Owners Loan Corporation; To lend money to home owners
5. National Recovery Administration; To regulate industry
6. PWA; Public Works Administration
7. SEC; To regulate the securities market
8. REA; Rural Electrification Administration
9. Agricultural Adjustment Administration; To regulate crop production

EVALUATING INFORMATION
1. T
2. F
3. F
4. T
5. T
6. F
7. T
8. F
9. T
10. T
11. T
12. F
13. T

MAIN IDEA ACTIVITIES 16.3

ORGANIZING INFORMATION
People earned money.
People had improved self-worth.
Class barriers were broken.

REVIEWING FACTS
1. drought
2. Agriculture
3. trees
4. Mexican Americans
5. Field Workers Union

6. federal government
7. Dorothea Lange
8. National Youth Administration
9. electricity

MAIN IDEA ACTIVITIES 16.4

ORGANIZING INFORMATION
1. *The Grapes of Wrath*
2. *Their Eyes Were Watching God*
3. *Native Son*
4. *Gone With the Wind*

CLASSIFYING INFORMATION
1. A
2. W
3. W
4. A
5. M
6. T
7. T
8. M
9. A

REVIEWING FACTS
1. *The Petrified Forest*
2. Lillian Hellman
3. Aaron Copland
4. *Grand Ole Opry*
5. Gospel music
6. Swing
7. regionalists

CHAPTER 17

MAIN IDEA ACTIVITIES 17.1

ORGANIZING INFORMATION
1. Five-Power Naval Treaty
2. Four-Power Naval Treaty
3. Nine-Power Naval Treaty

EVALUATING INFORMATION
1. F
2. F
3. T
4. T
5. T
6. F
7. T

MAIN IDEA ACTIVITIES 17.2

ORGANIZING INFORMATION
1. Emiliano Chamorro overthrew the Nicaraguan government, which started a bitter civil war.
2. The United States refused to accept Chamorro's government.
3. President Coolidge ordered the U.S. Marines to protect American commercial interests in Nicaragua.
4. President Coolidge sent Henry Stimson to negotiate an end to the civil war.
5. Stimson helped negotiate a peace treaty in May 1927.
6. Augusto César Sandino refused to accept Stimson's proposal.
7. Sandino organized a revolt against Chamorro and Adolfo Díaz.
8. General Anastasio Somoza ordered Sandino's assassination.
9. Somoza forced out the Nicaraguan president and took over the presidency.

REVIEWING FACTS
1. President Hoover
2. Good Neighbor policy
3. Cuba
4. United Fruit Company
5. nationalize
6. economic depression
7. Caudillos

MAIN IDEA ACTIVITIES 17.3

ORGANIZING INFORMATION
Hitler
prohibited Jews and non-Nazis from holding government positions
blamed Jews and Communists for Germany's decline
outlawed strikes
made military service mandatory

Mussolini
limited freedom of speech
arrested political opponents
restricted voting rights

Stalin
reorganized private land into farms run by the government
sent protesters to labor camps

UNDERSTANDING MAIN IDEAS
1. b
2. a
3. a
4. b
5. c
6. d
7. d
8. a
9. d
10. d
11. b
12. a
13. c
14. c
15. a
16. d

MAIN IDEA ACTIVITIES 17.4

ORGANIZING INFORMATION
pledged that the United States and Great Britain would not pursue territorial expansion
expressed that every nation had the right to choose its own form of government
called for freedom of international trade
called for equal access to raw materials for all countries

EVALUATING INFORMATION
1. T
2. F
3. T
4. T
5. T
6. F
7. T
8. T
9. T
10. F
11. T
12. F
13. T

CHAPTER 18

MAIN IDEA ACTIVITIES 18.1

ORGANIZING INFORMATION
Allied Advantages
tremendous manpower
great production capacity
enemy had to maintain troops on two active fronts

Axis Advantages
better prepared for war
firm control of invaded areas

CLASSIFYING INFORMATION
1. P
2. P
3. P
4. N
5. N
6. P
7. N
8. N

REVIEWING FACTS
1. Selective Training and Service Act
2. drafted
3. Douglas MacArthur
4. Japanese
5. Bataan Death March
6. Chester Nimitz
7. Battle of the Coral Sea
8. Battle of Midway
9. Stalingrad

MAIN IDEA ACTIVITIES 18.2

EVALUATING INFORMATION
1. F
2. T
3. F
4. F
5. T
6. T

UNDERSTANDING MAIN IDEAS
1. b
2. a
3. c
4. d

MAIN IDEA ACTIVITIES 18.3

ORGANIZING INFORMATION

1. The Allies left clues to make it look like the invasion would take place near Calais, on the English Channel.
2. The Allies landed in Normandy on June 6, 1944, with many troops.
3. The Allies bombed roads, bridges, and German troops.
4. Hitler refused to send reinforcements for the Axis troops.
5. The Allies had moved 20 miles into France by early July.
6. The Allies liberated Paris on August 25, 1944.

REVIEWING FACTS

1. Rome
2. sonar equipment
3. *Wehrmacht*
4. Operation Overlord
5. Holocaust
6. Battle of the Bulge
7. Yalta Conference
8. Japan
9. Adolf Hitler

MAIN IDEA ACTIVITIES 18.4

ORGANIZING INFORMATION

Tarawa
It gave the United States control of a vital airstrip.

Marshall Islands
The Allies were able to use airstrips on these islands to bomb the headquarters of the Japanese fleet.

CLASSIFYING INFORMATION

1. J
2. J
3. O
4. O
5. J
6. O
7. J

EVALUATING INFORMATION

1. T
2. F

3. T
4. T
5. F
6. T
7. T
8. F
9. T
10. T

CHAPTER 19

MAIN IDEA ACTIVITIES 19.1

ORGANIZING INFORMATION

planning the war
committing war crimes
committing other crimes against humanity
conspiring to commit crimes

EVALUATING INFORMATION

1. T
2. T
3. F
4. T
5. T
6. T
7. T

REVIEWING FACTS

1. Potsdam Conference
2. *zaibatsu*
3. Nuremberg Trials
4. Latin America
5. United Nations
6. General Assembly
7. Security Council
8. Palestine
9. Zionism
10. Israel
11. Ralph Bunche

MAIN IDEA ACTIVITIES 19.2

ORGANIZING INFORMATION

United States
democratic government
capitalist economy
belief in individual freedom

Soviet Union
use of force to overcome opposition

communism
government of one-party rule
suppression of religion
state-run economy

UNDERSTANDING MAIN IDEAS

1. d
2. a
3. d
4. d
5. a
6. b
7. c

MAIN IDEA ACTIVITIES 19.3

EVALUATING INFORMATION

1. T
2. T
3. F
4. T
5. F
6. T
7. T
8. F

CLASSIFYING INFORMATION

1. M
2. T
3. T
4. M
5. M
6. T
7. M

UNDERSTANDING MAIN IDEAS

1. a
2. d
3. b
4. c
5. a
6. b

MAIN IDEA ACTIVITIES 19.4

ORGANIZING INFORMATION

1. Loyalty Review Board
2. House Un-American Activities Committee
3. Internal Security Act
4. Religion

REVIEWING FACTS

1. National Security Council
2. Central Intelligence Agency
3. Hollywood Ten
4. Alger Hiss
5. Julius and Ethel Rosenberg
6. Joseph McCarthy
7. air-raid drills
8. *Sputnik*
9. *Explorer I*
10. National Defense Administration

CHAPTER 20

MAIN IDEA ACTIVITIES 20.1

ORGANIZING INFORMATION

Democratic Party
called for the repeal of the Taft-Hartley Act; an increase in federal aid for agriculture, education, and housing; broader Social Security benefits; and civil rights

Progressive Party
called for an extension of the New Deal and improved relations with the Soviet Union

States' Rights Party (Dixicrats)
called for continued racial segregation

EVALUATING INFORMATION

1. T
2. T
3. F
4. T
5. F
6. T
7. T
8. F
9. T
10. F
11. T
12. T
13. T
14. T

MAIN IDEA ACTIVITIES 20.2

CLASSIFYING INFORMATION

1. W
2. B

3. P
4. P
5. W
6. P

EVALUATING INFORMATION
1. T
2. T
3. F
4. F
5. T
6. T
7. T

UNDERSTANDING MAIN IDEAS
1. a
2. b
3. c
4. a
5. d
6. a

MAIN IDEA ACTIVITIES 20.3

ORGANIZING INFORMATION
Thurgood Marshall
argued against school segregation before the Supreme Court

Rosa Parks
refused to give up her bus seat to a white person; this led to the Montgomery Bus Boycott

Martin Luther King Jr.
a great leader for civil rights
urged people to fight back peacefully
spokesperson for the Montgomery Improvement Association

UNDERSTANDING MAIN IDEAS
1. b
2. a
3. c
4. d
5. d
6. d
7. b
8. d
9. d

CHAPTER 21

MAIN IDEA ACTIVITIES 21.1

ORGANIZING INFORMATION
John F. Kennedy
selected Lyndon B. Johnson as his running mate
Roman Catholic
Democrat
voters were impressed by his record of service during World War II

Richard Nixon
Eisenhower's vice president
Republican
chose Henry Cabot Lodge Jr. as his running mate
felt he had the maturity and experience to serve as president

REVIEWING FACTS
1. Twenty-second Amendment
2. Texas
3. television
4. John F. Kennedy
5. flexible response
6. developing countries
7. Peace Corps
8. African nations
9. Latin America
10. Fidel Castro
11. Bay of Pigs
12. Nikita Khrushchev
13. Berlin Wall
14. Limited Nuclear Test Ban Treaty

MAIN IDEA ACTIVITIES 21.2

ORGANIZING INFORMATION
John F. Kennedy
graduate of Harvard University
published two books
won a Pulitzer Prize
served as commander of a U.S. Navy patrol torpedo boat
suffered from Addison's disease

Jacqueline Kennedy
brought an appreciation of the fine arts to the Kennedy administration
organized a major restoration of the White House

Kennedy Children
the youngest to live in the White House since
  Theodore Roosevelt's presidency

EVALUATING INFORMATION
1. T
2. F
3. F
4. T
5. F
6. T
7. T
8. F
9. T
10. T
11. F
12. T

MAIN IDEA ACTIVITIES 21.3

ORGANIZING INFORMATION
Office of Economic Opportunity
Job Corps
Head Start Program
VISTA
allowed American Indians to establish poverty
  programs on reservations

EVALUATING INFORMATION
1. F
2. T
3. T
4. F
5. T
6. T

UNDERSTANDING MAIN IDEAS
1. a
2. b
3. b
4. d
5. a
6. d
7. b
8. c

CHAPTER 22

MAIN IDEA ACTIVITIES 22.1

CLASSIFYING INFORMATION
1. B
2. B
3. A
4. A
5. B
6. B
7. B
8. A

EVALUATING INFORMATION
1. T
2. F
3. F
4. F
5. T
6. F
7. T
8. F
9. T
10. F
11. T

INTERPRETING VISUAL IMAGES
1. Birmingham, Alabama
2. firefighters turning high-pressure hoses
   on young people
3. President Kennedy

MAIN IDEA ACTIVITIES 22.2

ORGANIZING INFORMATION
SNCC
organized registration of black voters in the
  South

Voter Education Project
provided money from private foundations to
  fund registration projects

COFO
conducted two mock elections to introduce
  voting procedures to African Americans

Freedom Summer
enlisted white volunteers from northern universities to help with registration projects

Voting Rights Act of 1965
placed the registration process under federal
   control

UNDERSTANDING MAIN IDEAS

1. c
2. b
3. d
4. a
5. c
6. a
7. d

MAIN IDEA ACTIVITIES 22.3

EVALUATING INFORMATION

1. T
2. T
3. T
4. F
5. T
6. T
7. T
8. F
9. F
10. T
11. T

UNDERSTANDING MAIN IDEAS

1. c
2. c
3. d
4. c
5. a
6. d
7. d
8. b
9. a

MAIN IDEA ACTIVITIES 22.4

ORGANIZING INFORMATION

harassment by the U.S. government
internal conflicts
decrease in financial contributions
organizations opposed each other's methods
opposition from white Americans

EVALUATING INFORMATION

1. T
2. F
3. F

4. T
5. T
6. F
7. T

REVIEWING FACTS

1. *Milliken* v. *Bradley*
2. affirmative action
3. *Griggs* v. *Duke Power Company*
4. quota
5. *University of California* v. *Bakke*
6. Carl Stokes

CHAPTER 23

MAIN IDEA ACTIVITIES 23.1

ORGANIZING INFORMATION

required that civil service hiring occur on the
   basis of ability, without regard to sex
made it illegal for employers to pay female
   workers less than male workers for the
   same job
created the President's Commission on the
   Status of Women
passed the Education Amendments Act, which
   outlawed sexual discrimination in higher
   education

EVALUATING INFORMATION

1. T
2. T
3. F
4. F
5. T
6. T
7. F
8. T
9. T
10. T
11. F
12. T
13. F

MAIN IDEA ACTIVITIES 23.2

CLASSIFYING INFORMATION

1. C
2. G
3. G

4. C
5. T
6. C
7. T

EVALUATING INFORMATION

1. F
2. F
3. F
4. T
5. T
6. F
7. T
8. T

UNDERSTANDING MAIN IDEAS

1. b
2. a
3. d
4. a
5. b
6. c
7. a
8. d

MAIN IDEA ACTIVITIES 23.3

ORGANIZING INFORMATION

American Indians of All Tribes

occupied Alcatraz and offered to buy the island for the same price as was paid for Manhattan Island

authorities removed protesters from the island

Wounded Knee

wanted renewal of American Indian culture and recognition of American Indian rights

the government agreed to consider AIM's grievances

Taos Pueblo Indians

recover 48,000 acres of land that was sacred to the tribe

their land was returned

American Indians in Maine

recover land in over half the state that had been taken from them

were awarded $81.5 million and the right to buy up to 300,000 acres of land

REVIEWING FACTS

1. poverty
2. self-determination
3. Ed Roberts
4. Rolling Quads
5. Rehabilitation Act
6. Education for All Handicapped Children Act
7. American Association of Retired Persons
8. Gray Panthers
9. Maggie Kuhn
10. Older Americans Act
11. Children's Bill of Rights

MAIN IDEA ACTIVITIES 23.4

ORGANIZING INFORMATION

casual
colorful
tie-dyed
women wore blue jeans
men wore longer hair
more men wore beards

EVALUATING INFORMATION

1. T
2. T
3. F
4. T
5. T
6. F
7. T

UNDERSTANDING MAIN IDEAS

1. b
2. d
3. c
4. a
5. d
6. d
7. a
8. c
9. c
10. b

CHAPTER 24

MAIN IDEA ACTIVITIES 24.1

EVALUATING INFORMATION
1. T
2. F
3. F
4. T

ORGANIZING INFORMATION
China
because of its agricultural abundance

France
for gaining access to Asian trade
in order to make new Catholic converts

UNDERSTANDING MAIN IDEAS
1. b
2. a
3. d
4. a
5. d
6. d
7. d
8. a
9. c
10. d

MAIN IDEA ACTIVITIES 24.2

CLASSIFYING INFORMATION
Doves
opposed the war
pacifists believed that war was wrong
felt that the United States was fighting against
the wishes of a majority of Vietnamese
felt that Vietnam was not crucial to national
security

Hawks
argued for more U.S. troops
supported the war's goals
wanted heavier bombing

EVALUATING INFORMATION
1. T
2. F
3. T
4. T
5. F
6. T

7. F
8. T
9. F
10. T

REVIEWING FACTS
1. Tonkin Gulf Resolution
2. escalation
3. 2 million
4. college deferments
5. 10,000
6. Operation Rolling Thunder
7. defoliants
8. Agent Orange
9. pacification
10. whites

MAIN IDEA ACTIVITIES 24.3

EVALUATING INFORMATION
1. T
2. T
3. F
4. T
5. T
6. F
7. T
8. T
9. T
10. F
11. T
12. T

ORGANIZING INFORMATION
Reasons
to produce a stable anticommunist government
to obtain peace with honor

Steps
troop withdrawals began in August 1969
gradual withdrawal of troops over the next
four years

UNDERSTANDING MAIN IDEAS
1. d
2. a
3. b
4. c
5. d

Main Idea Activities

MAIN IDEA ACTIVITIES 24.4

ORGANIZING INFORMATION

McGovern

deeply opposed the war in Vietnam

Air Force pilot in World War II

senator from South Dakota

Nixon

voiced a strong commitment to law and order

assured voters that the war would soon be
    over

EVALUATING INFORMATION

1. F
2. T
3. T
4. F
5. F

REVIEWING FACTS

1. Twenty-sixth Amendment
2. 1 million
3. East Meets West Foundation
4. 2 million
5. defoliants
6. birth defects
7. War Powers Act
8. Vietnam Veterans Memorial

CHAPTER 25

MAIN IDEA ACTIVITIES 25.1

ORGANIZING INFORMATION

Welfare

proposed the Family Assistance Plan

Southern Support

appointed conservative judges to the Supreme
    Court

delayed pressuring schools to desegregate

Economy

temporarily froze wages, prices, and rents

Energy Crisis

increased support for the use of nuclear energy

reduced the highway speed limit to 55 miles
    per hour

authorized the construction of a pipeline to
    transport oil from Alaska

REVIEWING FACTS

1. middle class
2. Family Assistance Plan
3. southern strategy
4. stagflation
5. Arab
6. Organization of Petroleum Exporting
   Countries
7. Environmental Protection Agency
8. Clean Air Act
9. Water Quality Improvement Act
10. Endangered Species Act
11. realpolitik
12. the People's Republic of China
13. détente

MAIN IDEA ACTIVITIES 25.2

ORGANIZING INFORMATION

Nixon's Pardon

Ford's popularity dropped

double standard

was agreed upon in advance

the full truth about Watergate would never be
    known

Clemency for Vietnam Draft Evaders

unfair to soldiers who had served their
    country

"We weren't criminals."

EVALUATING INFORMATION

1. T
2. T
3. F
4. F
5. T
6. T
7. T

REVIEWING FACTS

1. plumbers
2. Sam Ervin
3. Barbara Jordan
4. Gerald Ford
5. inflation
6. *Mayaguez*

MAIN IDEA ACTIVITIES 25.3

ORGANIZING INFORMATION
made Senator Mondale his running mate
took a new approach to government
said he would never lie or mislead the people
said he would make government decent, honest, and trustworthy

EVALUATING INFORMATION
1. F
2. F
3. T
4. F
5. T
6. F
7. T

UNDERSTANDING MAIN IDEAS
1. d
2. c
3. a
4. b
5. d
6. d

MAIN IDEA ACTIVITIES 25.4

CLASSIFYING INFORMATION
1. F
2. F
3. S
4. S
5. F
6. F
7. S
8. S
9. F
10. F

REVIEWING FACTS
1. Voting Rights Act of 1975
2. Bilingual Education Act
3. self-help books
4. rural
5. smokers
6. fast food
7. motion pictures
8. Steven Spielberg
9. disco
10. Neil Armstrong

INTERPRETING VISUAL IMAGES
1. computer
2. Answers will vary, but may include: by making people's jobs easier and improving communication, educational opportunities, and opportunities for recreation (for example, computer games). Accept all reasonable answers.

CHAPTER 26

MAIN IDEA ACTIVITIES 26.1

ORGANIZING INFORMATION
1. The United States helped overthrow Iran's leader and restore Shah Mohammad Reza Pahlavi to power.
2. Followers of Ayatollah Khomeini forced Mohammad Reza Pahlavi to leave Iran.
3. President Carter allowed Mohammad Reza Pahlavi into the United States for medical treatment.
4. Iranian militants took 53 American hostages at the U.S. embassy in Tehran.
5. In April 1980 a rescue mission failed when U.S. military helicopters crashed in the Iranian desert.
6. The hostages were freed on January 20, 1981.

CLASSIFYING INFORMATION
1. A
2. A
3. D
4. A
5. D
6. A
7. D

EVALUATING INFORMATION
1. T
2. T
3. F
4. T
5. T
6. F
7. T

MAIN IDEA ACTIVITIES 26.2

ORGANIZING INFORMATION

promised more freedom for the Soviet people

increased foreign trade

withdrew Soviet troops from Afghanistan

modernized Soviet factories

signed the INF

decreased military spending

REVIEWING FACTS

1. Grenada
2. Geraldine Ferraro
3. women
4. Sandra Day O'Connor
5. Gramm-Rudman-Hollings Act
6. Tax Reform Law of 1986
7. insider trading
8. Oliver North

MAIN IDEA ACTIVITIES 26.3

EVALUATING INFORMATION

1. T
2. F
3. T
4. T
5. F
6. F
7. T
8. T
9. F
10. F

REVIEWING FACTS

1. William Gibson
2. Christa McAuliffe
3. AIDS
4. Jesse Jackson
5. Republican
6. Soviet Union
7. Boris Yeltsin
8. Commonwealth of Independent States
9. Operation Desert Storm
10. women

ORGANIZING INFORMATION

Problem—rising costs; solution—make a reusable space shuttle

Problem—falling interest in missions; solution—send a civilian on a shuttle trip

CHAPTER 27

MAIN IDEA ACTIVITIES 27.1

ORGANIZING INFORMATION

Ross Perot

promised to decrease the influence of political lobbyists

promised to use his business skills to balance the budget

promised to give the public a greater voice in government

Bill Clinton

promised governmental renewal

George Bush

focused on the personal character of the candidates

CLASSIFYING INFORMATION

1. A
2. S
3. E
4. S

UNDERSTANDING MAIN IDEAS

1. c
2. a
3. c
4. d
5. c
6. b

MAIN IDEA ACTIVITIES 27.2

ORGANIZING INFORMATION

Event

white racists in Jasper, Texas, killed James Byrd Jr.

violence exploded in Los Angeles after four white police officers were acquitted of beating Rodney King

Response

called for tougher federal laws against hate crimes

launched the Initiaive on Race to encourage people to discuss racial issues and concerns

EVALUATING INFORMATION

1. T
2. T
3. F

4. T
5. F
6. T

UNDERSTANDING MAIN IDEAS

1. c
2. d
3. b
4. a
5. d

MAIN IDEA ACTIVITIES 27.3

ORGANIZING INFORMATION

Supporters

Immigrants create new businesses that help
the economy.

Immigrants have, on the average, more education than native-born Americans.

Opponents

Immigrants take jobs from native-born residents.

Large numbers of immigrants who are willing
to work for lower wages decrease wages
for all workers.

REVIEWING FACTS

1. Hubble space telescope
2. Shannon Lucid
3. John Glenn
4. Bill Gates
5. Internet
6. World Wide Web
7. Telecommunications Act
8. Family and Medical Leave Act

MAIN IDEA ACTIVITIES 27.4

ORGANIZING INFORMATION

Nuclear Power

People called for increased funding for
research on alternative energy sources.

Wildlife

The California Desert Protection Act converted two national monuments to
national parks.

Greenpeace campaigned against whaling.

Natural Resources

Recycling programs emerged.

EVALUATING INFORMATION

1. T
2. T
3. T
4. F
5. F
6. T
7. T
8. T
9. F
10. T
11. F
12. T

Main Idea Activities